FOUR CAREERS

FOUR CAREERS

AUTOBIOGRAPHY OF
CHARLES H. KRAFT

Foreword By Darrell Whiteman

WIPF & STOCK · Eugene, Oregon

FOUR CAREERS
Autobiography of Charles H. Kraft

Wipf & Stock
An Imprint of Wipf and Stock Publishers
199 W. 8th Ave., Suite 3
Eugene, OR 97401

www.wipfandstock.com

PAPERBACK ISBN: 978-1-5326-9942-9
HARDCOVER ISBN: 978-1-5326-9943-6
EBOOK ISBN: 978-1-5326-9944-3

Manufactured in the U.S.A.   10/22/19

CONTENTS

FOREWORD

By Darrell Whiteman

In June 1975 the American Society of Missiology, still in its infancy, held its annual meeting at Divine Word College in Dubuque, Iowa. The well-known Catholic missiological anthropologist, Louis Luzbetak, was president of the school and presided over the meetings. Gerald Anderson gave the presidential address. I was a graduate student in anthropology at Southern Illinois University at the time, studying anthropology as part of my preparation for cross-cultural ministry. I had recently read an article in the fledgling journal *Missiology* entitled "Dynamic Equivalence Churches" (January, 1973, vol. 1:39–57) by a young Associate Professor of Missionary Anthropology from Fuller Seminary's School of World Mission, by the name of Charles Kraft. I still have my heavily marked-up copy with lots of underlining and notes in the margins. This was one of the most exciting articles I had ever read as I was soaking up all I could to better understand how anthropology could relate to and serve God's mission in the world. I had been warned earlier as a young missionary in central Africa that if I studied anthropology I would probably lose my Christian faith, and even if I survived, anthropology had nothing at all to contribute to missionary work.

So imagine both my delight and intimidation to discover that the author of that great article, Charles Kraft, was attending the American Society of Missiology annual meeting. On the last night at dinner, I screwed up enough courage to introduce myself to Kraft, telling him how much I had enjoyed his article on "Dynamic Equivalence Churches." He graciously invited me to sit at table with him and for the next five hours, late into the night, I discovered a kindred spirit for life. He asked me the equivalent of "So, what do you want to do when you grow up?" I naïvely replied, "I want to become like *you* after I serve as a missionary for 20 years." Perhaps he was flattered, but he graciously invited me to come to the School of World Mission at Fuller as a visiting scholar. There I met another giant in the field of missiological anthropology, Alan Tippett.

I have often reflected on that "chance encounter" with Charles Kraft for it was indeed a Kairos moment, and it changed the trajectory of my life. It enabled me to connect anthropology and missiology in a way that would never have been possible without the 18 months I spent at the School of World Mission under the tutelage of Kraft and Tippett. Chuck was working on the final edition of his manuscript for *Christianity in Culture* and he invited me to give him feedback on what he had written. I read every page and many of them several times because it was such a creative and exciting adventure of interdisciplinary integration of cross-cultural theologizing. It was stunning. I also felt that in his creative thinking and writing Kraft was taking a risk and that this book would be controversial. I was concerned that conservative evangelicals with no knowledge of anthropology and linguistics or any understanding of cultural relativism would perhaps misunderstand Kraft's intentions and some might even brand him a heretic. After the manuscript was published by the Catholic missiological press, Orbis Books in 1979, I remember stating on more than one occasion that I thought this was the most important contribution to mission and missiology in the last 25 years.

My concern that the book would be controversial turned out to be true, fueled by a negative review titled 'The Cultural Relativizing of Revelation." by Carl F. H. Henry (1980, *Trinity Journal* 1 (Fall): 153–64), and an even less generous 100 page critique titled *Is*

Charles Kraft an Evangelical? by Edward N. Gross (1985, Christian
Beacon Press.) Both philosopher/theologian Carl Henry's and sys-
tematic theologian Edward Gross' severe critiques demonstrated the
very point that Kraft was making in his book, i.e., how our worldview
shapes our theology and biblical understanding and underscores why
philosophers and theologians have such a challenge to understand
and interact with missiological anthropologists because of their fear
and misunderstanding of the anthropological doctrine of cultural
relativism.

The Charles Kraft with whom I was interacting in the mid-
1970s was in his third career. It was his third career as a creative
and adventurous risk-taking missiologist that enabled him to
make sense of his first career as a missionary. That had ended pre-
maturely in disappointment, if not rejection by missionaries and a
mission board stuck in a colonial era mentality of colonizing pat-
terns of thought and behavior, and rejecting much of indigenous
non-Western culture.

Kraft's approach to mission was a "culture-affirming" approach in an era when indigenous cultures were too often seen
as the enemy, creating obstacles rather than stepping stones for
bringing people embedded in their culture and worldview face to
face with Christ. In his fourth career as a practitioner and theorist
of "power ministry" Kraft would discover that the Enemy is the
enemy, not culture.

The singular phrase that captures Kraft's understanding of
how God relates to human beings and therefore how we should
communicate and live out the gospel is "receptor oriented" communication. This may appear at first glance to be self-evident, yet
much missionary activity in the past and too much still today has
not taken seriously the cultural context of the receptor. Too much
emphasis has been on the message and the messenger and his or
her abilities rather than on the receptor's perceptions and understanding of what is being communicated. This receptor oriented
approach to communication is prefigured in the Incarnation where
God enters planet earth in the person of the itinerant Jewish rabbi
who we have come to know as Jesus the Messiah and savior of the

world. Therefore, Kraft takes both the Bible and culture seriously, recognizing that it is in and through culture that God has been interacting with human beings from the beginning of creation.

Charles Kraft will likely be remembered mostly for his fourth career focusing on God's power made available to followers of Jesus through the Holy Spirit. Reflecting on his first career as a missionary in Nigeria, he writes "I began to see that the biggest lack in our ministry was not the lack of cultural appropriateness, as I had been teaching. It was the lack of spiritual power." (p. 83.) Anthropology informed his cross-cultural awareness and sensitivity. The Holy Spirit empowered him to use the gifts of healing and deliverance. His ministry of inner-healing through his writing and practice has brought deliverance and freedom to many.

Have these paradigm shifts in the life of Charles Kraft been four disparate, disjointed careers? Not at all! With laser-like focus on God's desire to communicate with, transform, and empower human beings, Kraft has been a passionate servant of Jesus Christ for a long, rewarding, and fulfilling lifetime. This book will encourage all who read it to see how God takes us where we are on a spiritual and intellectual pilgrimage in order to transform us into what God wants us to become.

In this transparent and often vulnerable autobiography we see how God has used Charles Kraft, not in spite of his weaknesses, but often because of them to contribute to the kingdom of God throughout the world. Overcoming bouts of self-doubt, rising above criticism and misunderstanding from others, and propelled by a deep need to please his earthly father, Kraft has followed with a singular passion his desire to help people connect with God within their culture and with the power promised by the Holy Spirit. God has rewarded this creative risk-taker who has been swimming upstream much of his life with a long, productive and rewarding life. We as the readers are blessed to be able to see how a life given to God without reservations is unfolded with purpose and meaning, bringing empowerment and encouragement to thousands.

ABBREVIATIONS

AICC	Asian Institute of Christian Communication
CRI	Class of Religious Instruction
CT	*Christianity Today*
IRM	Intercultural Renewal Ministries
KSM	Kennedy School of Missions
MSU	Michigan State University
PA	*Practical Anthropology*
SIL	Summer Institute of Linguistics
SIM	Sudan Interior Mission
SIS	School of Intercultural Studies
UCLA	University of California at Los Angeles

INTRODUCTION AND OVERVIEW

WHAT YOU HOLD IN your hands is the story of a man who gave his life to be a field missionary in Africa, expecting to spend all of that life in Africa. But things got changed along the way. I am now eighty-seven years old and look back to see God's leading in four stages or careers.

I gave my life to Jesus at age twelve and have never taken it back, in spite of some disappointments and a good bit of wonder over what God was doing. But in each case when I was puzzled as to what He was doing, He used the puzzling things to move me in a new direction and a new experience of fulfillment.

I start with my beginnings. I was a small-town boy, a part of a lower-middle-class family living in Connecticut who met Jesus as a boy. I would say I was unremarkable, though I did fairly well in school and even skipped a grade.

Though none of my extended family had gone to college, somehow I grew to expect to go. Perhaps it was the fact that each of my parents felt they had been cheated out of college that led to their encouraging me to go. Perhaps they saw college for me to enable me to move up socially from their lower-middle-class position to an upper-middle-class one.

Then when Jesus entered my life and I felt a call to go to Africa, my aspirations began to sharpen. Church, college, marriage, seminary, mission board—all came into focus as I prepared and carried out my calling to my first career: *missionary*. This was very satisfying. And I would gladly have spent my life as a field missionary.

We loved the people. We were confident that our culture-affirming approach was the right way to go about our task. We never built ourselves into the church. It was theirs from the start and we were there to help, not to dominate. I refused to preach—that was their job. So were the details of running the church. They could do that, too. Only when it was necessary because of mission rules for an ordained person to officiate did I step in and take charge. Baptism and Communion were the main things that fell into this category.

But our approach was not the approved method of the Mission and, I believe was seen as a threat to their well-ordered, time-honored approach. So those in charge felt that our approach challenged them either to change or to get rid of us. They chose the latter. So we had to look for other employment.

We did not, however, give up seeing ourselves as missionaries. We were deeply hurt, very deeply hurt to have to leave the field. Our hearts were with "our people." So we looked for another missionary situation. But none that met our criteria turned up. So we decided that a secular position would be best until something in missions opened up.

So, without understanding what God was doing, we entered career two: *African language specialist*. When we found nothing that attracted us in the mission world at that time, I decided to accept the invitation offered by Michigan State University to join their faculty as an African language specialist. This would capitalize on the expertise I had achieved in Nigeria in the Hausa language, as well as make use of my training in linguistics and anthropology. We expected that this would be a temporary thing and give us opportunity to return to Nigeria from time to time.

So I finished up my PhD at Hartford Seminary Foundation and my wife, Meg, finished an MA and we headed to Michigan State and a new career: career two. This was a satisfying career but not vital. While at MSU I received a faculty research grant to collect and analyze data on the Chadic languages in Nigeria. Being in

Nigeria proved a great opportunity for our four children to experience the Nigeria we know and love.

This also gave us the opportunity to patch up our relationship with the Mission. The new leader of the Mission said, "We all agree with your culture affirming approach now." And he joined a couple of other new missionaries in taking a Hausa language course they asked my wife to teach.

It was near the end of our year back in Nigeria that I received an invitation to join the faculty of the African Studies Program at Stanford University. This would be a very prestigious position and I knew that any of my MSU colleagues would have jumped at it. I felt, however, that the informal agreement should be honored to return for at least one year to the institution that had given me the research year. So I wrote Stanford saying that I could be interested after I had completed the year I felt I owed to MSU. They didn't write back.

Then, back at MSU, I was given an invite to join a former professor of mine at Hartford Seminary who was now teaching at UCLA. What he offered was a "look-see" year at the end of which both we and they would decide if the position should be made permanent. This opportunity was attractive to us so I accepted it, asking MSU to hold my position there for a year away. So we headed to Los Angeles, where I spent the next five years (1968–1973) as an African language specialist.

Early in our year at UCLA we renewed our acquaintance with Ralph and Roberta Winter, whom we had taught with in a missionary training program before we (and they) had gone out to the mission field. Ralph was now teaching at Fuller Seminary in the School of World Mission. We had invited them for a Sunday dinner and found we had a lot in common as they worked in Guatemala and we in Nigeria. Toward the end of our time together, Ralph asked me if I would ever consider teaching in the School of World Mission. My answer was something like, "I gave my life to be a missionary, never expecting to do something else with my life. I don't think God has ever rescinded that call. Certainly I would consider it."

FOUR CAREERS

The result was a series of meetings with faculty and students where I got acquainted with the personnel at Fuller's School of World Mission, I made a couple of presentations, and I was offered a position on their faculty.

This was good but it faced me with a problem, since UCLA also had offered me a position. As I thought through my conundrum, I felt I could handle both tasks if I only signed up for part time at one school. So I approached my chairman at UCLA with the suggestion that I take the Fuller position full time and the UCLA position part time. He refused. He said they wanted me full time or not at all. He suggested, however, that if I took the UCLA position full time, whatever else I did would be okay and that he'd be glad to arrange my teaching at UCLA so I could handle this other commitment as well, as long as I met my obligations at UCLA.

So I went to Dean Donald McGavran, at Fuller, suggesting that I do part time at Fuller. He agreed. So from 1969 to 1973 I taught basically full time at both places, for half-time pay at Fuller.

This arrangement phased me into career three: *missiologist*, part time at first but full time from 1973 when I terminated at UCLA. I didn't really fit with the linguistic theory the UCLA faculty espoused. They gave me notice in 1972 that they were terminating me and that I would have one more year with them.

It was clear to me soon after I started at Fuller that my future lay with missiology. So the termination didn't bother me much since Fuller agreed to make my position there full time.

That first year, while I was teaching at UCLA, we lived in a "borrowed" house in West Los Angeles while the owners spent a sabbatical year in New Zealand. As soon as I began teaching at Fuller, however, we began looking for a house to buy in the Pasadena area, close to Fuller. Winter recommended South Pasadena as the city with the best schools, so we looked there and ended up buying a house near the high school.

For the next forty-one years, then, I got to do what God had been preparing me for. I was able to teach and write my culture-affirming approach to mission. Though I had enjoyed career two, it

4

was not vital. Missiology (career three) was and is vital to life and mission. I had found my calling and could teach on God and his relationship to humans within, not against, culture.

But God wasn't finished with me. In my thirteenth year on the Fuller faculty, God led me into my fourth career: *power ministry*. The year was 1982. We had gotten acquainted with a pastor named John Wimber. He had suggested we teach missionaries a course on healing.

I was interested because this was an area where I had failed as a missionary. People came who needed help and all I knew to do was to send them to a doctor or give them some medicine. I knew that Jesus healed a lot of people by faith. But I didn't understand that part of Jesus' ministry. When the Nigerians asked me what they should do about their biggest problem—evil spirits—I had no answer. My missiology was strong on culture but nonexistent on healing power.

So I attended Wimber's class, watching God use him to heal. I recognized that this was a missing piece of my faith and practice. I also knew that this dimension was missing in the approach of most of our students as well. When the administration no longer allowed Wimber to teach at Fuller there was no teaching on and practicing in this area, so Dr. Wagner and I decided to introduce courses in this area to fill the void. Introducing and practicing what I call "power ministry," then, has become my fourth career.

I will deal with these issues in more detail as we go along.

CHAPTER 1

EARLY LIFE

I WAS BORN AND brought up in Wolcott, Connecticut, a small town of perhaps three thousand inhabitants. We were so small that we had neither post office nor high school and both fire and police departments were volunteer. So we depended a lot on Waterbury, a city of a hundred thousand next to Wolcott. Born on July 15, 1932, in Waterbury hospital, I am the oldest child of Howard and Marian Kraft. My parents wanted another child, preferably a girl. I was joined on March 18, 1934, by Robert Alan Kraft.

Bob and I grew up together as the only children till I was ten (1942) when my parents tried again to have a girl but came home with David Peterson Kraft, born March 23, 1942. He was one of twin boys, named David and Daniel. But Daniel died five and a half hours after birth. Frustrated that they couldn't produce a girl, my parents adopted a sister for us five years later. Sharon Ann Kraft was born on August 1, 1947. She joined our family when she was six days old and she was everyone's favorite.

MY FAMILY

My parents, Howard Russell Kraft and Marian Augusta Northrop, had been high school sweethearts in the 1920s. Dad was the second of seven children in his family, four boys and three girls. His parents were American-born children of immigrants (father German, mother Swedish/Norwegian), lower middle class, doing their best to survive on a factory worker's salary. They were our grandparents, and they treated us well. We would go to their house on Christmas Eve and at various times during the year. I remember Grandma's pies, the card games of "Setback," discussions of athletics, especially how the Red Sox (or Red Flops) were doing. Grandpa tended to be quiet and Grandma in charge. They lived on a hill in the Waterville section of Waterbury. Waterbury was known as the "brass capitol of the world" due to the fact that there was so much brass manufactured there. One of these brass factories provided a salary for my dad.

Dad's mother was very strict with her children but we didn't know this till my mother told us about it when we were older, for they were very nice to us. When my dad and his siblings got old enough to work, Mom told us, Grandma required them to give all the dollars they earned to her. Their "allowance," what they got to keep, was the change.

Mom was the oldest of four girls, one of whom, Nita, the youngest, died at an early age. Her mother (Grandma Northrop, after Grandpa died, Grandma Hall) was an outgoing, outdoorsy type and Mom and her sisters grew up as girl scouts and athletes. Mom's father was an accountant/paymaster and a singer, a part of a local men's chorus called the Mendelssohns. They lived in the Mill Plain section of Waterbury, not close to the Krafts. Grandpa Northrop was almost fifteen years older than Grandma, and died of "elderly epilepsy" when I was four and a half (October 1936). I remember sitting on his lap on their front porch. They had a mountain ash tree in their front yard and I was fascinated by what I thought were the little oranges that grew on it.

My dad was a very good athlete (baseball, basketball, and, in secret from his mother, football) and a prize catch for any girl. He met my mother when they were both students at Crosby High School, class of '29, and they spent a lot of time together, often at her home. After graduation Dad turned down an athletic scholarship to go to college and instead went to work in one of the brass factories that we knew as Scovills. Mom entered a nurses training program in New York City but had to withdraw for health reasons. They got married on November 22, 1931.

MY EARLY HOMES

The question now was where would this young couple live. He was twenty, she nineteen. At first, they stayed in an apartment near Dad's parents. But Dad's mother's sister (Hilma) and her husband, Carl Peterson, had a farm in Wolcott, about six miles from the young couple's parents' homes in Waterbury. Great Uncle Carl offered the young couple a broken-down house on their property that was once owned by the parents of Seth Thomas, a famous eighteenth-century clockmaker. The house was inhabited by a multitude of small rodents, among other problems. It was offered on condition that they would make it livable. This they did, and I spent my first couple of years there.

In those days we had a dog named Jack, a St. Bernard/Collie mix who protected me ferociously. The mailman (or anyone else) was in grave danger whenever he got too close to my carriage when it was parked with me in it out in the yard. Jack was my best friend until he got hit by a car when I was nine. That was the greatest tragedy of my early life. I loved Jack and bragged about his ability to fight with and beat the dogs (German shepherds) from my uncle's farm and from the Churchelow's farm to the west of us.

Sometime in the early years of our stay in the old house, my parents made a deal with Uncle Carl to buy a piece of their farm to build a house on. Dad built a small house intended someday to be a garage and we moved in when I was about two. There my parents, brother, and I spent the next four years. My brother and I slept in the attic under the sloped roof of that house in good and bad weather.

While we were living in that house, my dad and various contractors worked to build another house right next to the one we were in. That house was completed in 1938. So, when I was six, we moved into the new house where I lived until I left for college (1949). From college days, to that house I would return for summers until I got married (1953). My parents lived there until my father died in the year 2000. Soon thereafter Mom sold the house.

I seemed to have a penchant for getting into scrapes. My mother nicknamed me "trouble." They told stories of me when I was only two or three nearly falling down into the hole Dad was digging to be the basement of the new house. At about the same age I fell down with a jar of beads and badly cut my hand. On another occasion when I was a bit older I managed to get into our car and release the brake and gearshift, nearly hitting my dad when the car coasted down into the cellar pit where he was working. At age two I was rescued from high up on a ladder.

Then, though it was not my fault, I had my front baby teeth knocked out when I hit the dashboard of my mother's car as she smashed into cousin Art's car on a curve just below the Peterson farmhouse when I was about six. I also fell out of my mother's moving car while trying to close the door when I was about eight. When I was twelve I cut myself badly on hand and knee trying to turn on a light over Great Grandfather Miller's museum showcase. I knelt on the edge of the showcase and broke the glass with my knee.

Grandpa Charles Sommers Miller, Mom's grandfather, was a historian, a blacksmith, and a locally famous leader of the Mattatuck Fife and Drum Corps. He was a family hero and it was in his honor that I had been named Charles.

THE WOLCOTT GREEN

Mom's mother, Grandma Northrop (she later became Grandma Hall after Grandpa Northrop died), was a favorite of ours. She collected things and taught all her grandchildren to collect things—stamps, coins, shells, Civil War memorabilia. If it could be collected, she encouraged us to collect it. I really got into stamp collecting from my teenage years and now have several valuable collections.

When Grandma Northrop was widowed in 1936, she scrambled to make ends meet by working as a nanny, then at a filling station store. She then remarried to George Hall, ten years her senior, and a distant cousin. He fascinated us. He lived in a Revolutionary War-era home on the green (the center of town) in Wolcott center and also had a home in West Hartford. We loved to visit them, especially at their Wolcott home, appropriately called "Juniper Ledge," where we could explore their large plot of land, including mower-cut paths through the trees and brush, a large area covered by a huge flat rock (the "Ledge"), and a home-made, spring-fed swimming pool down in the woods.

That pool holds a painful memory for me, stemming from when I did some work for Grandma and she gave me the choice of what I would be paid for the work. She said I could take money (about 25 cents, I think) or a swim in the pool or something else I don't remember. I really wanted the money but was ashamed to ask for it. So I opted for a swim in the pool, which I took, though the water was so cold I didn't really get to stay in long, and have regretted that decision all my life!

We had many a happy event at that house both before and after Grandpa Hall died early in 1946. We'd congregated there on holidays and had backyard cookouts between holidays. My brothers and I would do odd jobs for Grandma, usually helping her take care of the back yard, mowing grass (with a hand mower) and the paths down into the woods, gathering firewood, collecting food from her garden and the like—and playing in the woods and on the ledge. We probably weren't much help to her but we certainly enjoyed ourselves.

Also on Wolcott green was the Wolcott Congregational Church that we attended until I was twelve. And, in another corner of the green was the old Town Hall. I think they had stopped using that building for town business but they built an airplane spotting tower on top of it during World War II where they scheduled spotters, including my mother, to spot airplanes 24 hours a day as part of the "war effort." When I was about 11 or 12 I got to take a night shift to watch for planes. When we saw a plane, we called a telephone number to report the location of the plane and, if possible, identify the make of the plane. I doubt that we ever helped the war effort, but I certainly felt grown up to be entrusted with this opportunity to keep our air lanes safe!

Another thing they did with that building was to make a small basketball court out of its main room. We spent many hours playing basketball there.

SCHOOL TIME

For schooling, we were taken to school every day by bus. We had no kindergarten. Our town had several school buildings in various places around town. First, second, and third grades were in "New Woodtick," all in one room in Woodtick, a part of Wolcott. My teacher was Rita Fitzmorris for those grades. Fourth, fifth, and sixth, taught by Mrs. Finley, in "Old Woodtick," a single-room building about half a mile away from "New Woodtick." During the years I was in those grades (1941 to 1943), they had opened up that one-room stone school building because they needed extra space to hold all the children. That building had been built in 1835 as a one-room schoolhouse, but had been closed for years. There was a rumor that my Great Grandpa Miller had gone to school there years before me. It is now the home of the Wolcott Historical Society.

I did three grades in two years in that old stone building. I was a good student, except I was often in trouble for minor infractions. I did fourth grade normally but during fifth grade I got ahead of the class and, since sixth grade was in the same room and the teacher had an extra set of sixth-grade books, she let me use them to do sixth grade along with fifth. From about the middle of the year on, I was considered a sixth grader. However, whenever I would misbehave, I would get put back into fifth grade! When the end of the year came, I knew I would pass but I honestly didn't know if I'd be passed into seventh grade or into sixth!

To my delight, the teacher passed me into seventh, allowing me to be bussed to still another school, "North School," in another part of our town for seventh and eighth grades, taught by Miss Flahive in two rooms, one for each grade (the first time in my school experience I was in a room with only one grade in it.) These two years (1943 to 1945) passed relatively uneventfully and I graduated from eighth grade in the spring of 1945.

Starting in the fall, then, I was bussed to Crosby High School in Waterbury. My mother and father, as well as several other family members, had attended Crosby. My youngest uncle, Donald, was still in Crosby a year ahead of me and people thought we were brothers. I enrolled in a college prep course there and did fairly well academically, graduating number 66 of a class of 312 in 1949.

CHAPTER 2

GROWING UP

SPORTS

IN THOSE DAYS I went all over our town on my bicycle. When I was five or six I even ran away from home once on my bike. I don't remember what the problem was but I got about two miles away on the main road, without having packed food or clothing, before I was mercifully rescued by some concerned parents.

Often when I went out on my bike it was to play baseball or basketball with the other country kids. We played baseball from the time the snow was mostly gone in March till it covered the ground again in November. In the fall we played some football but mostly it was baseball, either arranged over our party line telephone with a bunch of other kids or, more often, with my brother Bob and/or one or two friends in the vacant lot next to our house (trying to avoid the cow flops left by the regular occupants of the lot). It was in that lot that I began to bat left handed for three reasons: (1) the right field wall (an ordinary stone wall) was a bit farther than the left field wall (it was over 180 feet), (2) the ball was easier to find if it went over the right field wall into another cow pasture rather than over the left field wall across the road and into the bushes on the other, and (3) my boyhood hero Ted Williams batted left handed.

In my earliest years, my dad played a lot of baseball and basketball. His baseball days were over by the time I became conscious of his playing but I can remember his last few years of basketball. He had been good enough at baseball to be offered a chance to try out for the New York Giants (so the rumor goes). With the depression on or barely over, he wisely turned that opportunity down. He chose the stability of a job and settled family over the vagaries of a professional baseball (or basketball) career.

I admired my dad very much and wanted to be an athlete like him. My mother was the dominant force in our lives as we grew up. The impression I had of Dad was that he really didn't like me. Unlike my brothers, I always felt ashamed in his presence, in spite of my admiration for him. I'm sure the impression of unwantedness was wrong but I believe it stemmed from him feeling trapped into marriage by the fact that Mom got pregnant before they got married. I have learned through counseling others of the importance of pre-birth memories in the formation of self-image. My self-image was not good and, I believe, the reason was my reaction to experiencing unwantedness before birth.

Perhaps if I did well in athletics, I reasoned, he would pay more attention to me. So I kept going out for the high school teams. In my freshman year, I stood 5'2" and weighed 120 pounds. I went out for the football team and they made me the water boy! Needless to say, I didn't make that team—or any other in high school, except for junior varsity basketball in my senior year and even then I seldom got to play. That Coach Lee allowed me to even sit there on the bench was, I believe, in recognition of the coach's esteem for my dad and his abilities rather than because of any ability I had. For me, I had college ahead and wanted to learn whatever I could by getting close to the players and coaches, so I was faithful at practices even though my chance of playing was remote.

The team I really should have made is the baseball team in my senior year. I was certainly good enough and had a good tryout. I perhaps could have made the team the year before, in my junior year, but I was sick (mumps, I think) when they had the tryouts. My take on not making the team in my senior year, however, is that Mr. Manherz, the baseball coach, was also the swimming coach who knew that I was a good swimmer and had tried to recruit me for the swimming team. I resisted, preferring my Dad's sports, basketball and baseball, to my mom's sport, swimming. But perhaps I was cut simply because the coach preferred to put his energies into underclassmen rather than to take on a senior who would soon graduate.

My mother was a swimmer and we were "brought up in the water," so to speak. She took us wherever there was water to swim in. She was an American Red Cross-certified swimming instructor and Bob and I did the various achievement tests my mother had devised before the age at which she and the American Red Cross had assigned for them. What this meant was that I passed the Junior Lifesaving requirements, designed for sixteen-year-olds at age forteen and had to wait two years for my badge. Likewise, I finished up the eighteen-year-old qualifications for Senior Lifesaving by age sixteen. Besides qualifying in lifesaving, we got to swim competitively at the YMCA and other places as well.

However, I got soured on racing when I came in first in a breaststroke race but was disqualified because I broke a rule I didn't know existed—that you had to make the final touch with both hands at once. I actually came in ahead of my brother, who got the ribbon for winning, because I only touched with one hand. I was about ten at the time and I only recall entering one more race after that experience. It was a long-distance race about that same year at the YMCA camp. It was for about three-quarters of a mile with several bigger boys in the race. I came in third, beating all but two of the bigger boys, and amazed everyone.

COMING TO CHRIST

Mom was lonely. Dad had a multitude of things that he did and left her alone a lot. She was an outdoors type, and full-time mothering and homemaking was not her "cup of tea." In 1936, when I was four, Mom was so discouraged, she decided to go down to the brook behind our house to drown herself. Life was just too demanding and lonely with two little boys to keep up with and no help from her husband who was out "doing his thing" to prove his manhood. So she decided to end it all. She told us she was out the door but providentially she returned to the house and reread a letter from her cousin, Enid Forsberg, who served as a missionary with the Sudan Interior Mission in Ethiopia and Sudan. Again, providentially, the letter outlined the gospel message as Enid and Mal presented it to Africans. Mom reread the letter and turned to Christ.

The decision to follow Christ changed things greatly for Mom. She began to carve out a life of her own, without focusing only on Dad and her loneliness, pouring herself into following Jesus and raising her boys.

With the hope of seeing my brother and me come into the same relationship with Christ, and, probably, for other reasons as well, our parents began sending us to various camps during the summers. We went to a YMCA camp (Camp Mataucha that had an Indian orientation) a couple of summers, to a liberal church camp in Massachusetts once and, in 1944, to Pineridge Camp in Rumney, New Hampshire, where we both made decisions to follow Jesus.

Having come to Christ, I felt I had to change churches. My Uncle Donald, my father's youngest sibling, only three years older than I, had found Christ and joined a small evangelical, missionary-minded church in Waterville, not far from Dad's parents' home. The church was named Waterville Union Church, carrying on in its name the fact that it had originated from the "coming out from among them" of a number of people from the liberal Protestant Congregational, Presbyterian, Episcopalian, and other churches in 1910.

It was to this church that we boys gravitated in 1945. Mom stayed in Wolcott Congregational Church for a few more years, visiting "our" church frequently, then joined us at Waterville Union (now Waterville Bible Church). Bob and I became part of their youth group and soon became leaders in the group. I began to grow rapidly in my faith, setting my alarm for 5:00 every morning so I could spend nearly two hours before the school bus came, praying, studying my Bible, and reading devotional, theological, and biographical books.

Under pastors Milton Nilson and, especially, John Samsvick ("Pastor John") I came to the conviction that I should give my life for service in Africa as represented by Enid and Mal, the cousins who had led my mother to faith. And there were two older maiden ladies and a Sunday School teacher who prayed for me and encouraged me to devote my life to missions. Mrs. Butcher, the Sunday School teacher, was especially influential. We young boys gave her a hard time with our cutting up. But she never stopped loving us and teaching us. The other two ladies were more in the background but their prayers were important factors in my life up through college days.

WORD OF LIFE CAMP

I spent parts of two summers during my high school years (1945 to 1949) at Word of Life camp. It was on an island in Schroon Lake, New York. The summer of 1947 was the first year that camp was open. The camp was run by Jack Wyrtzen, a New York evangelist who had developed a successful radio ministry. I had gone to camp that year (1947) for one week and stayed to work on the staff for the rest of the summer. These weeks contributed both to my spiritual growth and to my social life since quite a number of attractive girls came to camp too.

I worked initially on the work crew, digging holes for cesspools. Then, when they found out about my experience as a lifeguard, they made me third assistant lifeguard, several years younger than the other lifeguards. Once during that summer I swam around the island—three and a half miles—just to prove I could. I did a lot of surfboarding and some waterskiing that summer as well.

At Word of Life Camp, I gained a lot of maturity in my faith. I also met Jim Aberle, who would become my first college roommate, and Bob Dugan, whom we would add to the room our sophomore year. I also got to know several others who either went to Wheaton College or were planning on it. Among these were the members of a quartet who sang at Word of Life Camp during the summer but went back to Wheaton in the fall. Quite a number of the staff, speakers, and musicians recommended Wheaton as the place to train for missionary service. So I determined to go there for college.

I headed to Wheaton College in the fall of 1949 with one conscious and two semiconscious motives: to prepare for missionary service in Africa, to find a wife, and to become a good athlete to impress my father.

CHAPTER 3

PATH TO MISSION

TRAVELING TO WHEATON COLLEGE

It was September of 1949. In those days, my parents did not travel very far from home. Though they got over that eventually, up to that time my longest trip had only been about a hundred miles to either Boston or New York. So, heading to Chicago (nearly a thousand miles from home) and on to Wheaton was quite an adventure. The plan was for me to travel with my Uncle George and his wife to Indiana, then take a Greyhound bus to Chicago, and there catch an Aurora and Elgin train (the "Roarin' Elgin" we called it) to head for Wheaton.

I guess I should have been scared but I don't remember any fear of leaving home for a totally unknown destination. I guess I had imbibed my mother's attitude. When someone tried to console her for "losing a son," she turned on them saying, "Do you think I want him to stick around home and be a pantywaist the rest of his life?"

I know my leaving was a hard thing for Mom. She had depended on me to support her spiritually since Dad wasn't willing or able to do so. Mom and I used to pray together mornings before the school bus came. But, though the trip to Wheaton would be long and the surroundings strange, I looked forward to it as the next step in my pilgrimage.

Though the details of that trip are sketchy in my memory, I do remember the struggles of our oldish car pulling a house trailer climbing up the West Virginia mountains. This was before the Interstate Highway System, so the trip was mostly on secondary roads. But we made it to middle Indiana and were able to find the Greyhound bus station. I don't think I even stayed overnight before moving on. What has stuck in my memory is that it was 4:00 a.m. when I arrived in Chicago with my suitcases and I began my quest to find the Roarin' Elgin train. It may not have been far, though, because I think I walked, carrying a couple of heavy suitcases (before the days of wheels on suitcases). Soon I was on my way to Wheaton, got off at the right stop, and was met by my roommate-to-be, Jim Aberle.

FOOTBALL

One of the first things I did after arriving at Wheaton was to go out for the football team. When I appeared for practice, I was asked what position I played. I didn't know, since I had never played organized football before. But the coaches decided I should learn to play end and Art Johnston, the ends coach, and Chuck Holsinger, the line coach, took it upon themselves to teach me. I learned fast during our daily practices but didn't get to play at all in the first three "B" team (affectionately called the "Bombers") games.

I learned a lot in our scrimmages against the varsity, though, and my name was called to start the fourth B team game at end. And I started in the remaining games that season. Our varsity team was very good the year of 1949–50. We had a number of older men on that team—men who had been in the service during the Second World War and had come to school paid for by the GI Bill. However, our B team was pretty good also. We had several players who had distinguished themselves at the high school level, even a couple of players who had achieved all-state honors in high school. Then there was me, who had never played in high school. We regularly stopped the varsity in practice scrimmages.

We were better on defense than we were on offense in these scrimmages against the varsity. Playing end, on offense, I got to block either of two very large and strong varsity tackles, both ex-GIs, when we were on offense. Dick Simmons stood about 6'7", weighing about 280, Dale Oxley stood about 6'2", weighing about 230. But he was the tougher of the two. As I said, we did well until the coach got mad and yelled at us. Then I, at 180, often ended up on my back from trying to block the big men!

What I remember best, though, was a play I made on defense where I was at the bottom of the pile, having tackled one of our best varsity backfield men. As they unpiled us, I saw Coach Chrouser's face just above mine, shouting, "There's a comer, there's a comer."

I had a good time on the football team that freshman season. I've forgotten how many games we played but the fact that I was playing first string was deeply satisfying to me. But football wasn't the only thing in my life that year.

MEETING MEG

During the football season, we regularly got to the dining hall late after practice. So it was obvious to everyone in the dining hall who the football players were. As we went through the food line evening after evening I became attracted to one of the young ladies who was serving the food. She had large brown eyes and a very pleasant smile that seemed to invite attention. I determined to ask her for a date.

But there was a lot of competition. Meg went out with over forty different guys that year and would probably have dated many more if I hadn't been taking her out about once a week from late October to late January when she called it off and broke my heart!

I had become convinced that she was the one that God wanted me to marry and take to Africa. But I pushed her too hard. She had gone steady with a fellow in high school and did not want to be tied down so soon in college. On the walk between her dorm and mine after she told me our relationship was over my heart was broken but I got it straight with the Lord. I told him that I wanted him even more than I wanted Meg. And he gave me the assurance that we would get back together. So I decided to concentrate the next (sophomore) year on studies and making the baseball team and to try my best to let her go.

However, when the baseball season was over in June, it was the custom to have an outdoor picnic instead of a banquet for the team and our girlfriends. So I screwed up my courage and asked Meg if she would go out with me one more time before the school year was over—to the baseball team picnic. She agreed, I think with some hesitation, fearing that I might read too much into her willingness to accompany me. But we had a good time, after which I asked if I could write to her during the summer. She agreed to this also.

I went home for the summer and worked as a day camp counselor. Meg went to work at a Christian camp in Michigan. I wrote rather romantically. She kept each letter for a couple of weeks, then answered very unromantically about camp matters, tall trees, the beauty of northern Michigan, and whatever else was on her mind. I would respond immediately, grateful that she had written back even though she gave me no reason to be optimistic about our relationship. By the end of the summer, then, I resolved to try to put her out of my mind and focus on other things like football and studies.

WHAT TO MAJOR IN

During my freshman year I had begun to ask around to find out what major a prospective missionary ought to declare. Various suggestions emerged, but it was the suggestion made by an upperclassman who was headed for the Philippines as a missionary that made more sense to me than all the others. He said, "Anthropology, of course." When I asked what that was, he explained that anthropology was the only subject in the curriculum devoted to dealing with non-Western peoples. I was headed to Africa. So I decided to enroll in the introductory anthropology course in my sophomore year.

Marie Fetzer was our anthropology professor. She was a tough grader and I think I only got a B in her class. But I soon became enthusiastic about anthropology. Though we learned the basics of the discipline, I was attracted to the fact that she focused us on the application of the insights to missionary work. This was right down my alley. So, during my sophomore year, I declared myself an anthropology major.

BASEBALL

In baseball, I had done well playing right field on the B team in the spring of 1950. When spring of 1951 came around, however, I assumed that I would be on the B team again and so would not be invited to go on the southern trip, scheduled each year during the spring vacation. So, I arranged to take Meg home with me during the vacation to meet my parents. What a surprise it was to discover that coach Pfund had promoted me to the varsity and expected me to go on the spring trip! One of the tougher decisions I ever had to make in college was whether to carry out my plan to take Meg back to Connecticut during spring break or to scrap that plan and go on the baseball trip. I decided to forego the baseball trip, knowing that I would not play a lot anyway and that giving my folks the chance to get acquainted with my future wife was the more important thing.

So I went east with Meg rather than south with the baseball team. My folks, grandparents, and everyone else adored Meg and I was very pleased that I chose to take her home with me. I reconnected with the baseball team when we and they got back to school. Though I had been promoted to the varsity, as I suspected, I didn't get much playing time that year. It would have been so much more fun playing with the B team! Riding the bench in two sports, however, made a good sermon topic later, comparing my experience to that of the disciples who moved up to first string only after Jesus left.

MORE SPORTS

My junior year (1951–52) was a lot more fun athletically. I played first-string defensive end on the football team and got to play regular varsity right field in baseball.

Our main rival in those years was Lake Forest. They had an outstanding pitcher named Archie Jones. In one of our games against them that season on their field, I believe, he struck me out five times in a row! He had nineteen strikeouts all told, so I wasn't the only one striking out. Then, when we faced them again on our field, he struck me out two more times. As I was at bat working toward my eighth consecutive strikeout against Jones, coach Pfund called time out, came running down from his third base coaching spot, got in my face, saying, "Get down on your knees, close your eyes, stand on your head, do something you've never done before, but HIT THE BALL!"

Then he said something that changed my life. "If I didn't have confidence in you, you wouldn't be in the game. You're the best man I have for your position!" Then he turned and returned to his coaching position. I watched the ball all the way and doubled to the opposite (left) field!

The next year (1953), playing on their field, we faced Jones again. He was in good form and mowed us down. He only allowed us two hits, both mine: a single and a two-run home run! So, I felt that I had gotten back at him. Unfortunately, we lost to them 4-3.

Beyond the strikeout experience, I also got to play in a no-hit game in 1952. Dick Messner, arguably our best player, pitched a no hitter against Illinois College and I batted in four runs for him in the 8-0 win. I remember the pressure as the game went on and the fear that I might do something that would cost him his no hitter. That didn't happen and Dick got what up to that time was the only no hitter in the history of our conference (College Conference of Illinois and Wisconsin).

My senior year (1953) was a real challenge for me. In February I came down with a horrible pain in my stomach area. It turned out to be a gangrenous appendix producing fluid that was irritating my stomach. With the baseball season starting in late March, there was a serious question as to whether I would play this year. But little by little, I got into reasonable shape, though I was quite a bit weaker than normal. I went on the spring trip but in our first game, coach Pfund put my brother Bob in my spot in the lineup. I felt I could play but he felt he should be cautious. He did, however, put me in the second game and I did well enough that I played every game (except the first) that year and led the team in batting with a .290 average. Coach Corey, who wrote the history of Wheaton athletics (*Through Clouds and Sunshine Always*, three volumes, 1983) says I led the team in six categories.

CHAPTER 4

MORE PREPARATION

ANTHROPOLOGY

As a STUDENT OF anthropology, I studied the dynamics of culture. I also learned how important it is to respect and love a people for Christ by respecting their culture, the only way of life that makes sense to them. The fact that we were learning to use anthropology for the cause of missions made us the precursors of a movement to get cultural insight more prominently into missionary training.

In the fall of 1953 (after I had graduated) Dr. Robert Taylor, our main anthropology professor, founded *Practical Anthropology*, a journal that became a very influential vehicle for getting anthropology and communication theory into missionary consciousness. Published every two months, this little journal, at first mimeographed, contained seminal articles on the relationships between Christianity and the cultures of mankind. These were usually field-based, dealing with real life problems and how to solve them in ways that honored the people and were true to our faith. This was my first exposure to what I later called "Christian ethnotheology," a term I coined to label the culture-positive approach that I based my missionary activity and my academic career on.

Though the journal was started by Taylor, after a year or two it came to be supported by the American Bible Society and edited by Bill Smalley, who was then working for ABS in Thailand. *PA* became formative for me.

As I studied anthropology, played varsity football and baseball, and fell in love with Meg, I became attracted to linguistics and felt called to become a Bible translator. Linguistics was taught at Wheaton as part of an anthropology major, so I was able to take the equivalent of the first summer's course of the Summer Institute of Linguistics sponsored by Wycliffe Bible Translators as a part of my major.

These courses introduced me to the writings of Eugene Nida of the American Bible Society, who, in addition to his work in linguistics and translation, was pushing missionaries in various ways to study and apply anthropological insight to missionary activity. His lectures, published in 1954 as *Customs and Cultures*, were an important step in my movement and he became my hero. His writings in *Practical Anthropology* and the support of that journal by his office in the Bible Society were also significant.

I gobbled up the insights and approach to mission by Nida and the three perceptive "Bills" who worked with him: Bill Smalley, Bill Rayburn, and Bill Wonderly. These men studied what missionaries were doing and wrote much of it up in *PA*. Each had a keen sense of the way God does things in relation to the cultures of humans. We learned what we could by studying the mistakes and the successes of missionaries and their agencies. This was heady stuff but an incredibly valuable approach, as I was able to prove later.

LOOKING FOR A MISSION BOARD

During my senior year, we began to look for a mission board that would send us to Africa. We would have readily joined Wycliffe Bible Translators if they worked anywhere in Africa. Alas, they didn't at that time, and I felt called to Africa. So, I did a senior project (1952–53) in which I sent a form letter to about a hundred mission boards that worked in Africa, asking each their attitude toward sending someone trained in anthropology and linguistics to work toward Bible translation. To my dismay, the answers I received were not positive. None of the missions seemed to think of Bible translation as a specialty worth pursuing at that time. Some said they encouraged veteran missionaries to do translation. But none would appoint a newcomer with translation as his specialty. And not one was impressed with the value of anthropology.

Meg and I discussed our options thoroughly and ultimately decided that we should go to seminary. So I enrolled in Fuller Seminary and we lined up a job for her in Southern California in the area of her college major—physical education. Our plan was to get married when we graduated (June 1953), to move to California, and to continue our quest to find a mission board from there. We did, however, have one option to fall back on if nothing else developed.

My future father-in-law, Rev. Milton Bowman, was on the mission board of his denomination, the Brethren Church (Ashland, Ohio). That denomination was working in cooperation with the Church of the Brethren (Elgin, Illinois) in northeastern Nigeria. They had sent two couples and a single lady to participate in existing work with the Church of the Brethren and were anticipating manning and supporting financially a new work in northeastern Nigeria. This was the kind of situation we were looking for but we felt that it could not be God's will because it was too easy! Instead, we kept looking for a mission board and planned to go to Fuller until we found one. At that time there was no School of World Mission at Fuller. So we planned that I would study theology and especially the biblical languages in preparation for a career as a Bible translator.

However, Meg's dad never stopped telling us about this pioneer opportunity. So, one day Meg and I looked at each other and shared the fact that maybe we were wrong to keep looking when this opportunity was staring us in the face. Maybe this was God speaking to us. So we began to take the Nigeria opportunity seriously. I joined the Brethren Church and we decided to head to their seminary in Ashland, Ohio, instead of to Fuller. So I wrote them that I was not coming, and we made arrangements for housing and a job for Meg in the Ashland area.

A WEDDING

We got married on June 14, 1953. It was on a Sunday night, the evening before we graduated from Wheaton. The wedding was in the First Brethren Church in Nappanee, Indiana, a church that Meg's father had pastored for eleven years as she was growing up. The wedding had to be on a weekend so my folks could come from Connecticut for both graduation and wedding. The wedding was performed by Meg's dad.

The activity surrounding the wedding was a kind of foretaste of what our life would be from then on. We and our parents attended Baccalaureate in Wheaton on Sunday morning, traveled 180 miles to Nappanee, Indiana, for the wedding that evening, then back to Wheaton for graduation on Monday morning.

Then we headed southeast to Peru, Indiana, to Meg's parents' home, where they had taken a very full car of our wedding gifts. We spent a short time there opening gifts and then headed to our honeymoon place, Cook Forest, south of Erie, Pennsylvania. We then journeyed on to our summer's employment, running the craft shop at camp Sandy Hill, a boys' camp in Maryland. Neither of us had any special knowledge that would equip us for this job. So we learned by keeping one step ahead of the campers. We specialized in helping the campers make tooled leather purses, unborn calf wallets, and other things. And we swam, water skied, rode horses, and overall enjoyed ourselves.

ASHLAND SEMINARY

In the fall of 1953 I started seminary, one of a class of three! Meg got a job teaching physical education in a nearby town and we were accepted by the Brethren Mission Board as missionary candidates in training. Classes went well and I got mostly A's for grades—a big change from my B-minus average in college. I also assisted as a coach on the Ashland College football team. We did one year (1953 to 1954) with Meg working. Then the mission board decided to put us on support and ask Meg to take some education classes to qualify her to supervise elementary schools in Nigeria. So we moved to the missionary home, just off campus, and Meg took education courses plus Greek. This was ideal for us. We were put on salary and all we had to do was to study.

The summer of 1954 we spent at the Summer Institute of Linguistics / Wycliffe Bible Translators school at the University of Oklahoma in Norman, Oklahoma. I took the advanced course and Meg took the beginning course.

STARTING OUR FAMILY

We decided to start our family. The pregnancy went well but Meg got very large. So, at her sixth-month checkup the doctor remarked, "You're big enough for full term" and called for an x-ray. The x-ray found that there were two babies there. We were delighted that we would be a family of four going to Africa!

Meg finished her college classes at Ashland (struggling to fit into the classroom seats) a week before the babies were born (June 8, 1955). We went to the hospital when the birth was near and I sat in the waiting room reading a missions book (Lindsell's *Missionary Principles and Practice*) until a nurse came out and told me we had a girl (weighing 7 lb. 7 oz.) and a boy (weighing 7 lb. 1 oz.) and that all was well. I thanked her, asked when I could see Meg and the babies, and went back to reading, until I became aware of the silence in the waiting room. I looked up and explained, "We've known for three months that we had twins coming," and went back to my book.

During the summer of 1955, I took a couple of independent study courses at the seminary and helped with the babies. I was baptized by father-in-law Dad Bowman that summer and ordained as a Brethren elder in the Nappanee church. I also served

More Preparation

as interim pastor at Nappanee for three months, commuting each weekend by train from Ashland where I was continuing my studies.

Our, and the Brethren Mission Board's plan, was that we would finish seminary and at my request would take a year of mission studies at Kennedy School of Missions (Hartford, Connecticut), then head out to pioneer the new Nigerian field among the Kamwe (then known as Higi) people.

KENNEDY SCHOOL OF MISSIONS

After two years and an intensive summer of seminary, we were allowed by our mission board to delay the final semester of seminary and spend an academic year (1955 to 1956) studying at the Kennedy School of Missions in Hartford, Connecticut (a part of Hartford Seminary Foundation), taking linguistics, anthropology, African studies, and Islamics.

There were several things that attracted me to KSM. One of the top linguists in the United States, Henry Allan Gleason Jr., taught there. The top Africanist linguist in the country, William Welmers, was also on the faculty and I got to work with both of them. Welmers and I found a few Hausa materials that were available at that time. We worked together, giving me a head start on learning Hausa. It was a great year for us and, in addition to the very helpful coursework, I became a doctoral candidate with the expectation that after one year of study we'd go to the field and come back on our first furlough to finish the program. Meg was also able to take courses in anthropology and African studies.

Though we were on mission support, I needed to supplement our income. So I took a job as a night watchman, working from 11–7 (usually able to study during that time), going to class for several hours then to sleep in the afternoon for a few hours before going to work again. I also preached for three months for an Advent Christian Church in Plainville, Connecticut, that was between pastors.

In addition to my studies at Hartford, I was able to build a relationship with Eugene Nida, William Smalley, and William

Reyburn of the American Bible Society and to reconnect with Marie Fetzer, my former anthropology professor, whose marriage to Bill Reyburn had taken her away from Wheaton. We got to teach linguistics with Smalley one summer (1956) at the Meadville, Pennsylvania, missionary training program run by the Bible Society.

In those days, Ashland Seminary required a thesis as part of their BD (Bachelor of Divinity—now called MDiv) program. I decided to do mine on Islam in Nigeria. While at KSM I was able to take two courses on Islam from Dr. Kenneth Cragg, perhaps the leading Christian Islamics scholar. I informed him of my plan to develop my term papers from his courses into my BD thesis. So I wrote two forty-page term papers for him (one each semester), with the BD thesis in mind, incorporating Cragg's comments into the papers. I eventually added introductory and concluding chapters to round out the thesis before I submitted it.

During the academic year 1955–56 at Hartford, I decided to reach for a PhD with the expectation that I'd finish it on my furlough three years later. So I applied and was accepted to become a candidate.

DEVELOPING A NEW PERSPECTIVE

During my seminary years at Ashland, I took everything I could in Greek and Hebrew in addition to the regular curriculum, preparing for a career as a Bible translator. During this time Nida and Smalley, at the American Bible Society, assumed responsibility for the journal *Practical Anthropology*, and made it into a major influence in the lives and ministries of cross-cultural workers. I eagerly read and digested the journal as it came out every two months. I also was privileged to be one of a small circle of those who received prepublication papers by Bible Society men and women, sent out as "Translation Department Confidential Papers."

With only a semester's work to finish my BD, we returned to Ashland in the fall of 1956. I went to work taking my remaining classes and completing my thesis. I noticed something interesting, however. When the professors were attempting to answer students' questions, I could usually understand the professor and help him to answer the student! I believe it was the anthropological perspective, born at Wheaton, developed more at Hartford and in reading *Practical Anthropology*, that put me in quite a different position from my fellow students, even before we got to the field.

By early 1957, then, when the semester was over at Ashland, we were ready to head for Nigeria. We packed something like twenty barrels full of books, kids' clothing, and miscellaneous stuff that people had told us we would need in bush Nigeria.

As for the books, I remember asking Gene Nida what I should do with all my books—take them to Nigeria or leave them home. He said, "Take them with you. They might as well rot in Nigeria as in America!" So about twelve of the drums were full of books!

CHAPTER 5

BEGINNINGS IN NIGERIA

A LONG TRIP BY SHIP

WE PLANNED TO GO to Nigeria by ship (freighter) to see our loads plus some mission supplies through customs in Lagos. As we set sail on Farrell Lines "African Pilot" lots of friends and relatives were there to see us off. Ours was the first Farrell Lines ship to leave for Africa after a major dock strike and, contrary to regular practice, they just loaded all they could on our ship and sent it off to stop at eight ports. Ordinarily they would send one ship to no more than about three ports, but they wanted to get the loads off the docks, so they loaded everything they could onto our ship, destining us to a long trip with many stops.

Our first stop was Portland, Maine. After they loaded tons of grain, we were on our way across the Atlantic. A few days out, the smooth waters turned angry and we experienced a ferocious North Atlantic storm that lasted several days. Our ship pitched and dove and nearly all of us passengers and many of the crew got sick. This was a memorable experience for us travelling with twenty-one-month-old twins as waves washed over the bow of the ship, trunks slid from side to side in our state rooms, and dishes at meals slid across the table. We needed to cling to the railings to stay upright when walking. The captain was so shaken he took to drinking and was eventually put off the ship in Monrovia, Liberia.

The storm was eventually over and the rest of the voyage was quite pleasant. Freighters may be a slow way to travel but they are nice. There were only seven passengers—the four of us, a missionary couple, and a single woman related to a Farrell Lines staff member. Passengers are treated nicely and really get to know the ship's personnel as meals are eaten together. We often sat around with the crew hearing various officers relate their experiences of the sea. The crew did their best to spoil the twins. After meals the kids would go running to the officers' tables or to the stewards for handouts. Some of the crew gave them chewing gum which they didn't handle well.

We spent most of our time on the deck since it was so hot inside. The twins played, Meg wrote letters recording our experiences, and I read books (a total of eighteen!). What hurt the twins most was when we intently watched something over the high solid rail and they wanted to be held so they could watch, too. So we rigged up a deck chair and some cushions so they could sit and look over the rail, too.

We disembarked at most ports while the cargo was being unloaded, making new missionary friends who worked there, and doing some sightseeing. Our stops included Canary Islands (two ports), Sierra Leone, Dakar, Liberia, Ivory Coast, and Ghana (two ports). At last, after six weeks and eight ports, we were in Lagos, Nigeria, and so happy to disembark.

OVERLAND FROM LAGOS TO MUBI

It was the end of April 1957 when we arrived in Nigeria. We were met by a missionary who took us to the Sudan Interior Mission Guest House. We moved in with our suitcases, hot and sweaty, to wait for news concerning how to get our drums and get on our way north to Jos. Since we were not able to get our drums right away, and there was an SIM plane leaving soon, we decided to send Meg and our twins north by plane, while I stayed behind, waiting for our loads to be released and cleared through customs. So, we put them on the plane, planning for me to come a few days later with an SIM missionary in his VW bus with those loads that didn't fit on the plane.

After waiting about a week, until we determined that we could not predict when the drums would be released, we decided to take to the road. The next week or so, before I arrived in Jos, were quite a challenge for Meg. Though she was living in a fairly comfortable apartment in the Church of the Brethren compound, meals were served across the street in a dining hall at the SIM compound and she was alone with the kids. Various people were helpful but she missed my help. But at least the climate was better in Jos than it was in hot, muggy Lagos since Jos is at higher altitude and though warm, very pleasant. My two-day road trip was uneventful, but I got a good look at western Nigeria on our way to the northeast.

The plan was for us to spend a few days in Jos, buying the supplies we would need in the bush and then head by car the nearly five hundred miles of dirt road from Jos to Mubi where we would live for awhile to learn Hausa, the trade language. We would go with a veteran missionary, Clarence Heckman, in a comfortable Holden (Australian General Motors car built for bad roads) with whatever of our goods we could load on. Any further loads and, hopefully, our drums would be sent on later by truck.

When it came time to go, we prepared during the day and in keeping with mission custom, left at 6 p.m. to drive overnight to avoid the heat of the day. Though we could not have foreseen it, this was to be quite an adventure. We took off with me driving, telling myself continually to keep on the left side. (Nigeria now drives on the right, but in those days it was left-hand drive.) The road wasn't too bad from Jos for about eighty miles downhill off the escarpment. There was even potholed pavement on that part of the road, though it would be the last pavement we would see. We could go about 50 mph on that stretch. But when we lost the pavement, the road turned into a washboard, shaking our teeth mercilessly whenever the speedometer dipped below 40 mph. We found that if we could keep the speed above 40, the ride was smoother. But the road was such that because of the potholes we couldn't go long over 40. We probably averaged close to 35. Fortunately, there was virtually no traffic. I doubt if we passed more than a dozen vehicles in the whole five-hundred-mile trip. But there also were no service stations.

All went well as we descended from the Jos escarpment but when we were about 105 miles out, the car skidded off the left side of the road. One wheel was headed south, the other north and I couldn't control them. We got out and jacked up the car to try to find what was wrong and found a broken tie rod (the rod that connects the front wheels). When a tie rod breaks, it's almost always at either end. Providentially, as it turned out, this one was broken in the middle. Also, providentially, we were only about a mile past an SIM mission station.

But getting back to that station would be quite a challenge. Yet, the fact that the tie rod was broken in the middle meant we could splint it with tree branches, turn the car around and head back to the mission station. We used some rope we had bought for clothesline to take to bush. With two sticks and the rope we splinted the tie rod. This enabled us to turn the car back, then the splint gave way and we had to jack the car up again, get under the car and re-splint the tie rod. During one of these maneuvers the car fell off the jack, falling hard toward Heckman, bruising his arm. But we were thankful since he had just gotten out from under the car where he could have been killed. Again, the Lord was looking out for us.

This second splint held and we were able to drive very slowly the mile back to the SIM mission station. We drove in the driveway and woke up the single woman missionary who lived there. It was somewhere around 1:00 a.m.! We asked her if she would take us on to the next SIM station, about a hundred miles further on. She agreed. Heckman chose to stay at her station till he could hop a truck back to Jos. We would continue on in what has to be the most uncomfortable vehicle ever made—a World War II Jeep. Meg sat in the passenger seat with little Cheri. I got to sit on the metal seat over the back wheel, my head touching the canvas top of the Jeep, holding little Chuckie. Our loads were piled in on top of us. Though the seat gave Meg and Cheri some cushion, I got to feel every bump. If I remember correctly, we seldom got above 40 mph, the speed at which the bumps weren't so severe.

The good news is that we only had to do a hundred miles this way. We arrived at the next SIM station around 6:00 a.m. We were greeted by the man stationed there who agreed to take us the next hundred miles to the first of the Church of the Brethren Mission stations. It was extremely good news to us that he had a fairly new, large pickup truck that would be able to hold all of our loads in the back and both of us plus the twins not too uncomfortably in the cab. It took about two and a half hours to cover this last hundred miles and we arrived in Waka, the first CBM station, tired and dirty but very happy to have made it.

The next day, someone took us the next forty miles to the main CBM station—Garkida—where we stayed a couple of days before moving on another eighty miles to Mubi. The plan was for us to live in Mubi with Stover Kulp, the founder and field secretary of the Mission, who lived there alone after the death of his second wife. There we planned to find Hausa speakers and learn the language.

LEARNING HAUSA

Arriving in Mubi we unloaded the few loads we had with us, moving in with Dr. Kulp to learn Hausa. We then settled in for what turned out to be four to five months. Since we had linguistic training the Mission agreed that we could arrange our own learning program. Beyond settling into a new and very different place, we needed to begin working with one or more Hausa speakers.

We took over a round hut at the back of the property to serve as our office and learning place. I had collected in Jos several small books of fables and whatever grammatical and dictionary material I could find. I had also brought the Hausa grammar books that I had used with Dr. Welmers at Hartford.

We found a Hausa speaker named Ishmaila to come to our little hut daily to help us. So, we embarked on memorizing vocabulary in context and developing our hearing and speaking skills, first with Ishmaila, then going with him into the Hausa section of Mubi and into the market, using the Hausa we were learning. We focused on carefully learning the tones of each word, as the meaning varied if it was mispronounced. Soon we were going to the market without Ishmaila (we had Nigerians to help watch the kids, allowing Meg to go to the market as well). Little by little we got to understand a lot and eventually to speak a lot. But it was hard and by the time we'd been at it three months, we felt like quitting.

However, the mission leaders, eager to test our linguistic ability, had decided that after four months we were to begin teaching the language to four other missionaries. So we would have been shamed if we had come as linguists and failed in our first attempt. So, we trudged on and voilà, things clicked in after about four months. One day it seemed as though we'd never get it and the next day we were speaking the language! So, by the time the other missionaries came in late September, both Meg and I were fluent enough to work out lessons for them. Our plan was to work with them for a couple of months until they were at the place where they could work with language helpers on their own. Then we would go north to our station at Mbororo.

CHAPTER 6

AT MBORORO

IMPLEMENTING MISSION

BY DECEMBER OF 1957 we were ready to go to the newly opened station at Mbororo about forty-four miles north of Mubi, on the Cameroon border. This was to be our home base for the next two and a half years.

Our primary task was to learn the Kamwe (Higi) language, reduce it to writing, and begin a translation of the Scriptures. So, we began to work with a language assistant to learn that language. Though we got a good start, there were a number of important things that interrupted. For one, I was in charge of the four language learners back in Mubi. For another, there were Kamwe church activities, such as baptisms and examining candidates for baptism that took time. And I took every opportunity to visit Kamwe villages and to explore the area to get acquainted with the rapidly growing church work. So, the language work didn't go as fast as I would have wished. In fact, I chose to focus more on the church and neglected the Kamwe language learning, choosing to work in Hausa with the church leaders.

CHURCH GROWTH

The task of supervising the church work in addition to my language work put me in the position of adviser to a handful of very small churches. These churches had been started without much supervision, largely through the evangelistic activity of two local men: one blind and the other severely impaired by leprosy.

Giwa, the blind man, had trudged off to Kano (about 500 miles away) as a young man and enrolled in the Sudan Interior Mission's school for the blind. There he came to Christ and returned to his people as an evangelist, winning many to Christ.

The other man, Daniel, as a young man had contracted leprosy and was carried to the Church of the Brethren Mission leprosy colony near Garkida. This leprosy colony was eighty miles from his home in the Kamwe area. He lived there for several years and was living there in the fifties when a medicine that arrests leprosy (penicillin) was discovered and brought to the leprosarium. When his leprosy was arrested, then, he returned to the Kamwe area and was instrumental over many years in winning hundreds. Both of these men were received back by their people as having returned from the dead. Both welcomed us as we joined them in propagating the gospel.

As I got into working with the church leaders, it soon became evident that if the church was to grow in Kamweland, I would need to devote most of my time to aiding that growth. So, assuming that I could come back to the linguistic work later, I turned my full attention to working with the church leaders. These were really church planters but we called them evangelists or Christian religious instructors. So we began to find church planters and to match them with places that were requesting churches. When I took over supervision of the Kamwe churches, there were about four or five congregations (we couldn't find them all). Before very long, we grew that number to twenty or twenty-one!

The custom was to gain permission from a village chief to start a CRI (Class of Religious Instruction). If they were interested enough, they would build a mud brick building and an "evangelist" would move there to teach and preach. People interested in Christianity would attend these classes, and usually the Sunday service. During the classes, a certain number (often all of them) would commit themselves to Christ and "take the Covenant." This was our label for making a commitment to Christ. They would then enroll in what we called a covenant class—six months of instruction leading up to an interview that, if passed, led to baptism and full church membership.

The CRI teachers/preachers taught Christianity, literacy, and other secular subjects and established churches. My jobs included finding the preachers/teachers, training them, paying them (about 30 shillings per month), and, since I was the only ordained person, baptizing the converts when they finished their course and passed their interview. Our preachers/teachers were grown men who usually had completed Junior Primary School (4 grades) and did a remarkable job in a very receptive climate. So I soon found myself in what we learned later to call a "people movement." The growth was so rapid that, although converts had to go through the six-month training period before baptism, I was baptizing up to 150 a month! Not infrequently, being in the water that long meant that the bloodsuckers fed very well on white man's blood during baptisms until I began to wear hip boots!

A CULTURE-AFFIRMING APPROACH

Though the ground had been prepared and the receptivity was high, my culture-affirming approach probably had a lot to do with not stifling what God had already started through Daniel and Giwa. The approach I had learned at Wheaton and Hartford was surprising to the Nigerian leaders and very effective. The aim was that the local churches would never be under the control of the Mission. They were to belong to the nationals from the start and to be as culturally appropriate as possible. The Nigerian leaders got to do all the preaching, and in the Kamwe language. They asked me to preach but I refused. When they asked why, I stated that I did not want them to model their preaching after mine and, anyway, they should be speaking, singing, preaching, and administering in their language, not in Hausa.

An example of how I handled things was when the Kamwe leaders asked how many times I wanted to preach in the Mbororo church each month. I said, "None," though I was fluent enough in Hausa that I could have. They thought maybe I didn't understand and asked if I wasn't able to preach. I assured them that I could preach, and quite well. Then "did I want two weeks of the month or one." I still said, "None." So they asked me what I was planning on doing. I asked them what I could help them with. They had never been asked that question by previous missionaries, but they replied, "Bible study." So we arranged a date and I asked which of their homes we should meet in and what time I should come. They argued that their homes were not suitable for me to visit. They said they didn't even have a chair for me to sit on. I asked, "Where do you sit?" They replied that they sat on mats on the ground. I said, "That's where I'll sit." So I finally prevailed and we agreed to meet at the home of one of them and sit on mats.

We chose a book of the NT to study and read a chapter. They then looked at me and asked, "What does this mean?" I replied, "I don't know." They asked if I had never read the passage before. I assured them that I had but that I didn't know how they would interpret the passage. This surprised them. "Of what importance is our interpretation?" they asked, "The missionary always tells us what the passage means!"

I explained that I'll do things differently. "I'm not going to tell you," I said, "because I don't know how you understand it. And if this is to be your church, it will be yours from the beginning and based on what you understand of life and the leading of the Holy Spirit." From then on, the question was "What does this Scripture mean to you?" not simply "What does it mean?"

I did my best to keep from being in charge, helping and teaching the leaders. I wanted them, the Kamwe leaders, to be the ones who actually led the church.

So, they did the evangelizing, grassroots teaching, and examining converts for baptism in their own language (often done in other areas by missionaries). I had let the leaders know that, since I didn't know Kamwe, they could say things that I couldn't check up on. So they were accountable only to God for what they preached and taught. I limited myself to teaching the leaders (in Hausa) and baptizing. And the church in our area grew faster than the mission leaders believed a church could grow, making them suspicious of what I was doing. I taught mostly informally in these weekly Bible study meetings but at one time I had all the village preachers come in for a two-week Bible school. I also met with the pastors monthly for discussions on topics concerning their work, the Bible and what they would preach on. They learned a lot and I learned a lot.

Reports from the Kamwe church leaders to date estimate that the Kamwe tribe of some 750,000 or more people is now over 95 percent Christian. I believe that a combination of the work of the early evangelists and our culture-affirming, local-control approach are the main human reasons for this church growth. The Holy Spirit, of course, was the main reason for the growth, using this approach, however, had a lot to do with it.

FAMILY MATTERS

Life was going smoothly and we had adjusted to no electricity, cooking on a wood stove, boiling and filtering all our water, growing our own veggies, watching out for snakes, etc., when we decided to expand our family. Things went well with the pregnancy for a couple of months when Meg started having some problems in her midsection. I elected to take her to the Mission hospital in Lassa for the doctor to examine her. I chose to take her on my motorcycle because it had better suspension than the Jeep. I judged that it would be less rough and, therefore, less of a threat to her pregnancy. The doctor was speechless! He read me out in no uncertain terms over my choice of vehicle, not buying my reasoning. The doctor examined her and decided to operate to repair an umbilical hernia. Though she was pregnant, he assured us that the repair would not be endangered as she grew larger. The operation went well but he made me go back to Mbororo and return with the Jeep to take Meg back home.

The pregnancy went well but her due date in October made things chancy in relation to the rainy season (April to early October). The problem was the quarter-mile wide Yedseram River that we had to cross, about a mile from the hospital at Lassa. During the dry season (October to March) locals constructed a "drift" (a sticks-and-stones crossing over the dry river) that allowed us to drive the fifteen miles to Lassa in about an hour. But when the rains came hard and the river rose to about eight to ten feet deep with a strong current, we could no longer drive across it and had to go about fifty miles via other roads to get to Lassa. If we stayed home till she was ready to deliver, we would probably have had to go the longer route and might not have been able to get there in time. So, come mid-September, we went to Lassa by the long route and I left Meg and the kids there to live with a missionary nurse, until the baby came.

When I visited Meg during the month she was living there before Ricky was born, I would come to the bank of the river on my motorcycle, park the cycle in a home there, undress, and with my clothes held high in one hand, wade and swim to the other side. I could walk about one-third of the way across, then have to swim against a strong current for perhaps fifty yards till I could touch again on the opposite side. Though I am a strong swimmer, I never was able to land where I planned—the river was too strong and I would end up quite a ways farther down stream. I would then shake myself as dry as possible and put my clothes back on— often with several interested Nigerians looking on.

As we got closer to the due date, I stayed at Lassa, helping Meg with the kids and waiting. Richard Lee was born October 14, 1958, and I was present and able to hold him even before Meg did. Three-year-old Cheri and Chuckie, who had been waiting at Lassa with Meg for so long, were excited and even tried to walk to the hospital by themselves (perhaps a quarter mile from the house they were staying) to see the newcomer. Fortunately they were intercepted and got to see him soon after. Some time later Chuckie, who was always coming up with questions, asked, "Why isn't he black like all the other babies?"

Things returned to normal for a few months, then one day I noticed that Cheri's eyes looked quite yellow and she seemed quite listless. When the doctor came on one of his regular visits to our dispensary, we had him examine Cheri. He determined that she had contracted hepatitis. He said, though, that we should stay at home where we were at Mbororo, rather than moving to the hospital at Lassa, lest others catch it from us, but to watch ourselves lest we also come down with it. Cheri's cleared up in about three weeks, but then Meg came down with it. When she had had it for about three weeks, I came down with it. Mine also lasted about three weeks. I guess we were lucky that our cases were mild, compared to what some others experience. However, I have never felt so weak as when I had hepatitis.

People often ask what was our most difficult experience in Nigeria. It's not hard for me to answer that. Undoubtedly it was when Ricky, a toddler of fifteen months, drank kerosene mistaking it for water. I had gone in our car to Mubi to teach Hausa to some of our missionaries, leaving Meg and the kids behind without transportation. One evening a missionary from Lassa came with bad news. His words were, "Chuck, hop in your car and get to Lassa as quickly as possible. Little Ricky has drunk kerosene and we're not sure he's going to make it!" I obeyed with a very anxious heart. "Why, God? Have I done something wrong that you're punishing me? Why pick on the little guy? If I'm at fault, let the bad stuff happen to me."

The distance to the Lassa hospital from Mubi was about forty-four miles. This was the longest forty-four miles I've ever traveled. I questioned God about half of the way. This was the special little guy I had watched being born and held before his mother had. We so looked forward to our upcoming furlough and the chance to show him off to our relatives. Now, the thought of losing him was the greatest pain I had ever experienced. There were other times when God seemed distant but this was the worst and I cried and questioned about half of the way to Lassa. Then I came to what I always came to—God is there and he cares. He cares for Meg and little Ricky, who must be going through a lot more than I am right now.

At Mbororo, where Ricky discovered a can used for putting kerosene into the cooling mechanism of our refrigerator, Meg found him coming out of the pantry fighting to breathe. Smelling the kerosene she figured it out and tried to get him to throw up, until she found Dr. Spock's book that instructed her not to make him throw up because that exposes his lungs to the fumes a second time. So, she held him, praying as he gasped for breath, going long times without breathing and scaring her. What to do? She had no car or telephone available. She sent for the Nigerian dispenser and the school headmaster, Dandi, who owned a motorcycle. Together they decided the solution was for Dandi to go as fast as he could (it usually took the better part of an hour to travel the fifteen miles of deeply rutted dirt road to Lassa) and get the doctor to come to Mbororo. So, in about an hour and a half, the doctor arrived, gave Ricky some penicillin and pumped his stomach. That hour and a half was filled with prayer and short breaths with long pauses between breaths. And fear that Ricky might not make it. Once the doctor was there and Ricky's stomach pumped, they decided to take Meg and the twins to Lassa so the doctor could keep an eye on Ricky. As they traveled to Lassa, Meg's job was to keep Ricky awake. Thankfully all worked out and we were able to introduce a healthy baby to our relatives a couple months later. Praise to God.

CONFLICT WITH THE MISSION

The fact that I worked with rather than against the culture brought us into conflict with the mission leaders. We encouraged indigenous music, Christian dances, "untrained" church leadership, decision-making by them, the use of traditional drums and other instruments, and forgiveness rather than punishment for those who had sinned. And we were vocal concerning our belief that it was unbiblical to exclude believing polygamists from baptism and church membership. Though these things made our relationship with the mission leadership rocky, we enjoyed the trust and support of most of the Nigerian church leaders both within and outside of our area.

One result of this trust was that at the Majalisa (area church council) meeting in 1959, I was elected to the Mission Church Committee. This was the joint missionary-nationals supervisory committee, made up of two-thirds nationals, one-third missionaries. National delegates came mainly from three tribes—Bura, Margi, and Kamwe. They were over the total Church of the Brethren area. At this meeting, my name was put up by the Nigerians against that of the missionary field chairman to be elected to a place on this committee. I had no input in this or even knowledge that my name would be put on the ballot, but the Nigerians elected me to a three-year term on that committee, in spite of the fact that I was to go on furlough within a year. This event showed the mission leadership that my popularity with the Nigerians was a threat to their system.

LAST DAYS IN NIGERIA

In the spring of 1960 it was decided that we'd pack our things for furlough (due to start in May 1960), take a minimum of stuff with us, and move again to Mubi to start another group learning Hausa. I was to teach three couples Hausa and Meg was to look after their children as well as ours. Our Mission was starting a school that combined agriculture with Bible near Mubi and these missionaries would need to speak Hausa to carry out that new venture.

At one point during this time I was asked to speak to the class. I remember talking about how Jesus accepted outcasts and applied the principle to the acceptance of believing polygamists, among others. A missionary's Nigerian cook heard about this and created a fuss over it.

This class at the Bible school was my last opportunity to make my position known to the Nigerians. Looking back, I probably shouldn't have chosen that topic and that illustration to speak on, even though I was (and am) thoroughly convinced that the Mission position is wrong.

My position did, however, get carried on by the Kamwe pastors after we left. One of them got to be secretary of the church council and regularly, year after year, put dealing with the polygamy issue on the agenda. Fourteen years after we left the field, in 1974, the council finally dealt with the issue and decided, as reported in our Brethren Church magazine, that the Nigerian church "will now accept people into membership on the basis of faith alone." I thought this was one of the reasons for our being there in the first place!

THE LAST STRAW

As mentioned above, a major issue between us and the mission was the fact that we opposed the mission policy against baptizing believing polygamists. We were in a pioneer area, working in a society that required polygamy of its leaders. Culturally, a leader in order to be accepted as a leader must prove himself by handling well a home with more than one wife in it. So, observing in Scripture that God was patient with this custom, we advocated that we ought to follow God's lead rather than Western sensibilities. The mission leaders were adamant against our position. They recognized only the first wife and considered polygamy to be immorality, blaming the husbands for being oversexed and unfaithful.

Working within the culture made us sympathetic toward those who wanted to follow Jesus and join the church but were excluded. We knew that the Kamwe, like Africans in general, simply had a different definition of marriage. Their definition enabled every woman to be married, since there are always more marriageable women than men. The missionaries also didn't know that the primary advocate for a man taking a second wife was his first wife, who enjoyed the help and fellowship she got from a second woman in the household. Working in a pioneer area, we found there were several men (often leaders) who came to Christ who were excluded from church membership simply because they followed their custom and were too honorable to kick out second and third wives.

With the polygamy issue and several other issues in mind (e.g., a church tax on those who wished to take communion and the excommunicating of church leaders who had gotten into moral trouble and then repented for shorter or longer periods of time depending on the supposed gravity of the sin), I requested a meeting with the field committee (at that time all missionaries) shortly before we were due to go on furlough. My question to the field committee was, given my feelings on the issues, were we invited back after our furlough? I was a brash twenty-seven-year-old and undoubtedly offended them with my attitude. I remember telling them in a meeting with the mission leaders, "If you can prove from the Bible that the mission position is correct, I'd give my life to defend that position. But if you can't prove your position from the Bible, I'll fight it as long as I live!" The meeting ended with them saying they would allow me to come back if I promised to fight things within acceptable guidelines. I ended by saying that I've never done otherwise and I've never knowingly baptized a polygamist.

We had one more interview (the night before we left Jos for furlough) with the chairman of the mission. He spent a couple of hours questioning us and trying to get us to accept and support the mission position on a number of cultural issues. The discussion was not a happy one, but we were invited back and left with the expectation of returning. But before we had been home two weeks, a letter came saying that the field committee had changed its mind. So, in spite of what looked like success in our work (the Kamwe church had grown greatly), we were told we could not return after our furlough.

CHAPTER 7

AFRICAN LANGUAGE SPECIALIST

REENTRY

WE FLEW WITH OUR three kids in a four-engine propeller plane
(a DC6) from Kano, Nigeria, to London. It took twelve hours!
After another twelve-hour flight to New York on a DC6, it was
pure delight to be met by our relatives and spend a few weeks in
Connecticut with my family.

The most memorable thing that happened while we were in
Wolcott was the letter we received from the mission saying that
we were not to return to Nigeria after our furlough. This was a
real blow, given the fact that the field committee (made up totally
of missionaries) had specifically said that we were invited back.
But the reversal of that decision was to be final. Over the next
few weeks, though, we had conversations with the Church of the
Brethren general secretary, who was about to go to Nigeria to
check on the work. He assured us that he disagreed with the field
committee's decision and that he would investigate and would attempt to get us back on the field.

We don't know what happened on that trip but he wrote us
when he returned that the field committee's decision was final but

refused to give us any further information. So we were cut loose from the Church of the Brethren Board but remained under the Brethren Church Board. They sided with us.

Probably the fact that Meg's dad was on the Brethren Church Board had a lot to do with the decision of that board to stick with us. They let us know that they would financially support us both in the upcoming year of schooling at Hartford and under any other mission board that we might choose to link up with.

The summer of 1960 I had, however, committed myself to teach in the Toronto Institute of Linguistics, sponsored by the American Bible Society, which, under Eugene Nida, sponsored missionary-training seminars under culturally savvy missiologists such as Bill Smalley, Bill Reyburn, and Don Larson. TIL ran for two months in June and July and provided the context in which I could interact with these men whom I considered giants in approaching mission in the culture-positive way that I used and that got me fired. Associating with them helped greatly in encouraging me in the rightness of our approach and the value of the teaching and writing from that perspective that God was leading me into in years to come. Beyond TIL, then, our summer was spent in connecting with relatives and friends, arranging for housing at Kennedy School of Missions in Hartford, and whatever else we needed to do to get ready for the coming years at KSM.

KENNEDY SCHOOL OF MISSIONS

The next three years, from fall of 1960 to spring of 1963, were spent at KSM completing my doctorate. KSM in those days was the nearest thing available to what I was later involved in at Fuller School of World Mission. KSM had been started after the big Edinburgh missionary conference in 1910 and was the premier missionary training school in its day.

In returning to KSM after three years in Nigeria, I was disappointed to find that my major professor in African linguistics, William Welmers, had moved to UCLA. But, since I had been admitted to a PhD program, I decided to stay at Hartford. Al

Gleason, one of America's top linguists, and several other faculty members well-known in their fields were still there. Gleason asked me to become his teaching assistant to conduct the lab sessions that went along with his introductory linguistics course.

In the year 1960–61 I completed the coursework and comprehensives for my PhD. Since I was focusing on culture as well as linguistics, I did comps in both linguistics and anthropology. I also passed exams in French, Greek, and Hebrew. An exam in Hausa was also required and Welmers was contacted to find out who could give the exam. His comment was, "It is my understanding that if someone is to be examined in Hausa, it is Kraft who gives the exam!" Before we left Nigeria, I had taken an exam given by another mission and passed it at what they estimated was about a six-year level, though I had only been there three years. KSM accepted that as my exam for Hausa. Having passed the exams, I got down to work on my dissertation. It was to be "A Study of Hausa Syntax."

From close to the start of our 1960–63 Hartford days, we began attending the West Hartford Baptist Church. At first, we were feeling spiritually and emotionally pretty wrung out. So we had decided to try to keep quiet so we would not be noticed and could just absorb what the church and pastor had to offer us. This "traveling incognito" lasted for a few weeks only. We were asked then if we would work with the youth of the church. We answered, "Okay," and began to meet with the junior highs. This was a neat, though challenging, volunteer experience from 1960 to 1963.

We had been advised by the doctor in Nigeria that if we wanted another child, we should plan to have the child in the United States. Meg had had more bleeding than normal with Rick's birth and, while the doctor did not advise against another pregnancy, he did feel that we should have the resources of a US hospital available just in case. We did want another child. Karen Louise was born without any problems in Hartford Hospital on May 22, 1961. She was a delightful child and we all were thrilled to add her to our family.

Another thing that happened was that it occurred to me that we might be able to pull Meg's various graduate studies together to get her an MA. KSM had just instituted a two-year, non-thesis MA. So I took a look at Meg's transcripts and decided to take them to someone who could tell me if she could get a degree. She had elementary ed credits plus Greek from Ashland, the Wycliffe linguistics credits from the two summer courses she had taken at the University of Oklahoma and some courses she had taken from KSM before our Nigeria experience. The upshot of this query was that she only needed sixteen more semester hours to complete a sixty-unit MA program. And we had two years to do it in. Four credits in each of the four semesters would do it. Either I or the lady across the hall from our apartment could look after the children while Meg was in class. This we did and she was able to get her MA at the same time that I was granted my PhD (June 1963)— with four children looking on!

I was to graduate in June of 1963. But a glitch appeared. A grant for $2,000 of tuition that the school had promised was never put through. So, by their accounting, I owed them $2,000 and couldn't graduate until that was paid. With no resources, I calmed my anger and went to a bank to borrow the money, not knowing if the bank would allow me to borrow. Fortunately, they granted my request and I was in debt for the second time in my life. The first was in Nigeria where I had taken a loan from the Mission to buy a motorcycle. I remember taking the check to the KSM finance office and saying to someone that I would rather have contributed to them as a happy alumnus than to have them take my money this way. I vowed I would never contribute to Hartford Seminary Foundation. And I never have!

WHAT TO DO NEXT

One of our major concerns during the year 1960–61 was to figure out what we would do when I finished my PhD. As mentioned, our Ashland Brethren Church Board had promised to support us if we would find another mission to serve under. I corresponded with

Eugene Nida of the American Bible Society, who offered us a position in Latin America. This did not appeal to us, since our experience had been in Africa. Wycliffe would have been our first choice but they didn't work in Africa yet (they did later). Nevertheless, in the summer of 1961 we had returned to the Summer Institute of Linguistics at the University of Oklahoma at Norman to pursue the possibility of working under Wycliffe Bible Translators in the opening of their work in Ghana.

During this summer, we applied, were interviewed, and were accepted as candidates-in-training with Wycliffe, with the aim of joining their team in Ghana when my work at Hartford was finished. We hoped at that time to be able to complete the dissertation within a year. We had some misgivings about going to Ghana where the languages are of quite a different family from Hausa. But we applied anyway, with all our doubts, and were accepted.

The next year at Hartford went well, though we were frustrated that my project was taking so long. The summer of 1962 was spent teaching Hausa at Michigan State University. It was the day of the National Defense Education Act that sought to develop expertise in languages that might be needed in the future if a crisis developed in their regions. Hausa was on the list. Centers were set up in various universities to train people in these languages. Michigan State was one of the universities that had, with government help, set up an African Studies Center. It was also the day of the Peace Corps. MSU was deeply involved in training Peace Corps volunteers and others who wanted to learn African and other languages (sponsored by other centers), often on government grants. At Welmers's suggestion, MSU invited me to teach Hausa that summer in a Peace Corps program.

We gladly moved for the summer to Lansing, Michigan, where many of Meg's relatives lived. We were able to rent a house from her aunt, living in the house ourselves and providing a small apartment in the back for Benji, our Nigerian Hausa-language helper.

This stint resulted in an invitation to join the MSU faculty as a member of the developing African Studies Center, with Hausa as my specialty. They wanted me to come right away and to finish my dissertation while teaching. I wisely turned them down, pending the completion of my doctoral work. The emergence of this opportunity, however, competed with our desire to return to Africa. But the only opportunity at that time was to go with Wycliffe to Ghana.

We prayed fervently about this decision and without being quite sure why, we felt that God wanted us to take the position at MSU rather than going back to Africa (Ghana) with Wycliffe. So we resigned from Wycliffe and assured MSU that we would be available the following year (1963), after I graduated.

One of these summers, after I started at MSU, I taught Hausa at Syracuse University with Tony Kirk-Greene, who got me involved in writing *Teach Yourself Hausa* (1973), a reference grammar. Tony had been working on it and had done most of a draft of it. But, since he respected my knowledge of Hausa grammar and tones, he turned it over to me and I finished it up. I also taught a Hausa course at UCLA one of these summers.

MICHIGAN STATE UNIVERSITY

On completion of my degree in June of 1963, we headed for Lansing, Michigan, with our faithful station wagon loaded to the gills, pulling a large rented trailer. I think we only passed one or two vehicles all the way from Hartford to Lansing! Everybody else passed us! We arranged to live in Meg's folk's house in Lansing. The rent was only $120 per month.

I was offered an $8,000 salary by MSU. This sounded pretty good to me since it was double what we had been living on for three years. I was to be a part of the Languages Department (later called Linguistics) and the African Studies Center. My job was to teach Hausa at whatever level, plus other linguistics courses. In the process of teaching, I continued what I had begun in Nigeria, developing teaching materials that were eventually published. At first, we only had introductory-level students but in my second and succeeding years I had intermediate and eventually advanced students. I was also able to develop an adjunct relationship with the Anthropology Department and to teach the Language and Culture course for them.

In moving to MSU, I joined two other faculty members specializing in African languages. In addition to Hausa, we taught Swahili, Yoruba, Igbo, West African Pidgin, Bambara, Fulani, and maybe another one or two that I don't remember. I was able to bring on several former missionaries as adjuncts to teach some of these languages. Our students consisted of those who majored in African languages, usually on government grants, plus others, including missionaries. We also were able to meet in our home regularly with those students who were missionaries in training at MSU for informal sessions dealing with culture, communication, and other missionary issues. Included in that group was the missionary couple who succeeded us and lived in the house we had built in Mbororo, Nigeria.

In addition to my regular professorial responsibilities, I was involved in several Peace Corps training programs, both at MSU and in other places (e.g., Boston University). Meg was also able to teach introductory Hausa in some of the Peace Corps programs.

One of the promises that had been made to us when we were considering MSU was that we could get back to Nigeria under their sponsorship. So I got to take several trips to Nigeria plus a year's research under MSU auspices. I attended a language conference in Freetown, Sierra Leone, in 1963 and was able to get to the other side of Africa (Kenya) in 1964. In addition, Meg and I shepherded a group of twenty-five to thirty MSU students to the University of Nigeria, at Nsukka, during the summer of 1964.

CHAPTER 8

ANOTHER YEAR IN NIGERIA

In 1966 WE WERE able to return to Nigeria for a year. I had applied for a government research grant plus a research grant from MSU to collect data on small languages related to Hausa. Both grants came through, so we sublet our house, arranged for housing in Nigeria and made all the other necessary arrangements, packed to be gone for a year and took off. We lived in Jos while I was collecting word lists in sixty-five languages, all but three related to Hausa.

On the trip out, the six of us spent several days in Geneva, sightseeing. We stayed in a very special hotel room overlooking the fountain on Lac Leman (the lake of Geneva). We did various touristy things, including a boat trip to the northern end of the lake and back plus a cable car trip up one of the Alps.

The sightseeing over, we thought, and the money we had set aside for the trip about finished, we checked out of the hotel and headed by taxi to the airport. As we checked in at the airport, however, we hit a snag. Though we knew little French, the phrase "coup d'etat" got our attention. There had been a coup in Nigeria and our Swissair flight was not going. "Until when?" I asked. But they could not tell me. What to do? Six of us stranded! We had checked out of our hotel and were nearly out of cash. We returned to the hotel and, fortunately, they had room for us.

After spending another four days, we got the telephone call we were hoping for and so headed by taxi to the airport. Apparently things had settled down enough for air travel to start up again. So, we flew to Nigeria on what I believe was the first plane in from Europe after the coup. We disembarked with machine guns trained on us but got through customs and other formalities in record time, since it was after dark and those checking us through were probably more scared than we were.

THE BIAFRA WAR

A few weeks after we moved in, the riots that culminated in the Nigerian civil war erupted. The issue was that the Igbos, the major southern tribe, had killed the northern leader and taken over the government. This was followed by a reverse coup that put a northerner back in power, enabling the northerners to rebel broadly against the Igbos that still had power in the north. The message the northerners were sending to the Igbos was that if they didn't leave and go back to "their place" in the Eastern Region (though for many the north was the only home they had ever known) where their people came from, they would be killed. Many of the Igbos left, but many had stayed, apparently thinking the northerners weren't serious with their threats. Some of the Igbos were arrogant, even calling the northerners "monkeys" or other insulting names. These were the ones who were the target of the killings, though many others got caught up in the rioting as well.

The rumor was that there were at least ten thousand people killed in Jos where we were living and more than that in some other cities. It was a horrible time. Another rumor was that the killings were targeted at the Igbos first, the Yorubas second, and then the whites. There was nothing we could do but wait it out. At one point, a severely wounded Igbo who had fled the rioters turned up on our porch. I prayed that he would leave but he didn't. Instead, he pleaded with me saying, "I'm a Christian, you're a Christian. If you don't help me, I'll die right here!" I didn't know what the risk might be for myself or my family, but I knew I had to help him.

So I bundled him into the back of my pickup, hoping that none of the rioters would see him, at least until we had passed them, not knowing whether taking him to the hospital would mean help or death for him. The news broadcasts spoke of the rioters going into hospitals and hacking every Igbo to death.

As it turned out, this man got to safety. So did another man who turned up on "our property" the next day. But he was not wounded. What I elected to do was to leave this man in our compound while I went to the police station to ask them to send a policeman back with me as protection. I would then drive him to the police station where people were congregated in an enclosure waiting for transport out of the area. At the police station, a sergeant ordered a corporal to go with me and he refused! After a few minutes, however, he agreed and we went back to our compound, retrieved the man, and headed back to the police station. On the way, the policeman said to the Igbo, "You owe your life to this man." The Igbo replied, "I know it."

When the riots were over, it became obvious that they were not about genocide but, rather, were an attempt to chase the Igbos out of the region. If it had been genocide, as some in the world press reported, the rioters could have killed hundreds, perhaps thousands more at the police station where hundreds had congregated or at the hospital where many wounded were being treated. As it was, those who got to the police station or the hospital were safe and were trucked or flown south. Since many of them had grown up in the north or lived there for many years, they were being "returned" to places they had never known.

The riots were over in October. The riots seemed to be turned on one day and off three days later. But the violence calmed down, giving way to political maneuvers. We were untouched by the fighting, though, and I was able to get started on the research that our sponsors were paying for.

RESEARCH

My research was to collect language data on Chadic language (largely small, unwritten languages related to Hausa) that fill Nigeria's "Middle Belt." I was able to hire a young man from a missionary family whose ability in Hausa was impressive to assist me in the data collection.

In the year we were there, we were able to record 134 words and phrases in sixty-five different languages. We were amazed that we were able to collect that much data in one year, especially with what else was going on in the country. Our best sources of informants in these languages were the leprosaria run by various missions where people of many different tribes were living. These word lists were eventually published in Germany in 1981 in three volumes with tentative phonemic analyses done by myself and students at UCLA.

In the spring, following unsuccessful negotiations, war broke out in the south. However, though there was always the threat of it coming our way, it never did. So I was able to do my research virtually without interference from political events.

REBUILDING OUR RELATIONSHIP WITH THE MISSION

During this year we also were able to rebuild our relationship with the Mission and to assist them with language instruction and advice on other issues. The new field director (there now was no field committee) approached me to ask if I would help the Mission by teaching Hausa to some of the Brethren missionaries. I replied that I was to work full time on the research I was sent to conduct but that I would ask Meg if she would teach them. She agreed and did two courses while we were there, one of which the field director himself attended.

He also asked if I could help the missionaries convince the Nigerian pastors to baptize believing polygamists! Given our history, I was stunned by this question and asked him to repeat it. He smiled and said, "I know why you were not allowed to come back. But we all agree with you now!"

STANFORD?

Another thing of interest that happened during this year was an invite to move to Stanford for a year that could result in a permanent position. I would work with Joseph Greenberg, a prominent Africanist linguist of those years in a very prestigious position. This was tempting and would have been jumped at by any of my MSU colleagues. However, there was an informal rule that if a university gives a person a year to do research, that person owes the university at least one year after returning. I took that expectation seriously and told Stanford that I'd consider it for the following year but that I felt I had an obligation to spend the next year at MSU. They never repeated their request.

I've often wondered how different our lives would have been had we accepted that offer. We probably never would have gotten to Fuller and Biola and I would have spent the rest of my academic days dealing with African languages rather than missiology. How often God's leading looks like chance!

UCLA

Shortly after we returned to Michigan State, an invitation came for me to accept a position in African languages at UCLA. It was to be a visiting position at first with the possibility of permanence. Bill Welmers, who briefly had been my supervisor at Hartford, was now at UCLA and wanted me to join him in that prestigious African studies program. So we accepted the invitation and planned to move there in the summer of 1968. As it was, UCLA was to be my academic home for the next five years, enabling me to publish several works on Hausa and Chadic languages in addition to teaching.

At UCLA I taught various levels of Hausa plus courses on language teaching. I did research on African languages, especially those related to Hausa on which I had collected data during our 1966–67 year in Nigeria.

It was on a Sunday in early 1969 that we invited Ralph and Roberta Winter and family to come and have a meal with us. As I mentioned in an earlier chapter, we had met them while teaching in a missionary training program in Meadville, Pennsylvania, in 1956. I had also met Ralph at an Urbana Missionary Conference in 1967, after they had returned from Guatemala and he had started teaching at Fuller. I remember him talking excitedly about the School of World Mission and the potential impact that new school would have on missions. I listened and got excited for him. But at that time California seemed a long way away.

We had a very pleasant afternoon with Ralph and Roberta. Toward the end of that time, Ralph asked me a life-changing question: "Would you ever consider teaching at Fuller?" Recovering from the shock, my answer was something like, "God once called me to be a missionary. I don't believe he has ever rescinded that call. Yes, I would consider it." Within days, I was asked to come to Fuller to meet the faculty.

I met Donald McGavran, the dean, whom I had read but never met. His book *Bridges of God* had been sent to us while in Nigeria by the home board. I remember reading it and thinking, "At last someone is taking a pro-culture position. More power to him." Then I met Alan Tippett, the SWM anthropologist. I had only seen a short article of his in *Practical Anthropology*, and had no idea at that time of the depth and breadth of this man. These two plus Winter made up the SWM faculty. They seemed to be likeable people and I could see myself getting along with them quite well if things worked out.

Then on another visit, I was invited to speak to the students and discuss with the faculty the possibility of my joining the Fuller faculty. At one point in this process the faculty asked me to discuss polygamy. I remember thinking that my views on polygamy would keep me from being accepted by them, but I had to be honest and tell them what I thought. Unknown to me, they had already published an edition of the *Church Growth Bulletin* that took essentially the same position I took. So, contrary to my fears, what I said on the subject was taken positively by them.

The Fuller faculty was also impressed by my 1963 article in *Practical Anthropology*, entitled "Conversion, Cultural or Christian?" In that article I had contrasted conversion that required a major cultural change to be similar to requiring Westerners to move from one culture to another as a condition of salvation. Mc-Gavran liked my approach so much that, once I joined his faculty, he assigned me to teach a whole course entitled "Conversion with a Minimum of Social Dislocation."

Things proceeded from there and soon I was invited to teach at Fuller. So I went to the chairman of the UCLA Linguistics Department, asking if I could teach part time at UCLA and full time at Fuller. He said, "No, we want you full time. But we could arrange your classes so you could do other things on certain days. Just don't tell us what you're doing." So I went to Dr. McGavran at Fuller and asked if I could teach part time for Fuller. He said, "Yes." So, for the next four years I taught full time at UCLA (on Mondays and Wednesdays) and also full time at Fuller (on Tuesdays and Thursdays) but on a half-time salary at Fuller. Each place had faculty meetings on one Friday per month. Seldom did the faculty meetings occur on the same Friday.

MOVING TO SOUTH PASADENA

In the spring of 1968–69, we needed to think about where we would live the following year. We would have to move out of the house we were renting when the owners came back from New Zealand. We had committed ourselves to joining the Fuller faculty and saw our future there with our position at UCLA as temporary.

So we began house hunting in the Pasadena area. We found a very large one in South Pasadena that we liked. The house had an uncanny likeness to the one we were renting in West Los Angeles, with lots of room for our children to grow up in. With a bit of fixing, each child could have his/her own bedroom. South Pasadena had both good schools and a small town atmosphere.

So, I resigned from MSU where I still had a position and we moved to South Pasadena. We enrolled the kids in South Pas schools and began a new life in Southern California. At UCLA, though I continued to do an acceptable job in the classroom, my heart was no longer in African languages and linguistics. So between 1969 and 1973 I finished up and published my *Introduction to Spoken Hausa* (1973), with Meg as coauthor, *Teach Yourself Hausa* (1973), with Tony Kirk-Greene, and *A Hausa Reader* (1973). I also worked out (with student help) before leaving UCLA the tentative phonological analyses of the sixty-five languages included in my three-volume *Chadic Wordlists*, though that wasn't published until 1981 with financial help from Fuller. Thus, by 1973 I had wrapped up my career as an African language specialist. Now I could be a full-time missiologist at Fuller (and for full-time pay).

CHAPTER 9

THE FULLER YEARS: 1969–2008

MY BEGINNING DAYS AT FULLER

MY MOVE TO FULLER was the most satisfying career move of my life. I couldn't have been happier. I had found my niche, an opportunity to teach my culture-affirming approach to mission, and not to neophytes. In those days our students had to have three years of field experience to be accepted into our programs. At one point we found that our students averaged forty-two years of age and fourteen years of field experience. It was challenging and exhilarating to be dealing with experienced people all the time helping them to do their jobs better.

We had only about thirty-five to forty students in those days, so we got to know many of them quite well. Meg and I had most of our students to our home, couple by couple, for a meal in the first few years of my time at Fuller. On one occasion we had a middle-aged couple with us for Sunday dinner. When they had left, our kids asked, "Who were those people anyway?" Meg answered, "They're some of Daddy's students." With a very puzzled look on her face, Cheri asked, "How can they be his students? They're older than he is!"

The first course I was asked to teach was introductory anthropology. The area I cut out for myself at Fuller was the relationship between Christianity and culture. As I've mentioned, one of the first new courses I taught was entitled "Conversion with a Minimum of Social Dislocation." This course was to spin off from my 1963 article on conversion in *Practical Anthropology*. Over the years, I developed other courses on what I labeled Ethnotheology (a cross-cultural approach to theology), Indigeneity (the church in culture), Contextualization, Christianity in Culture, Intercultural Communication, Anthropological Theory, Ethnolinguistics, Worldview and Worldview Change, and Bible Translation. I also did an Africa area course and a course on African Independent Churches.

BIOLA TEACHING

Before I get into the substance of my Fuller career, let me say a few words about my relationship to Biola University. As I was completing my stint at UCLA in 1973, my fourth year at Fuller, the chairman of the Missions Department at Biola University (who was doing his doctorate with us) came to me asking, "Would you help us by teaching the introductory anthropology course at Biola?" Since I was used to teaching at two places and had terminated my position at UCLA, I agreed, on condition that they look at Meg as a possible full-time faculty member. He agreed and for the next four years I taught the anthropology course at Biola each Monday evening for three hours. It drew about eighty students the first time (Fall 1973) and went up from there. Meg taught two courses amounting to a half-time position for each of us. Then, in 1977 Meg finished her doctor of missiology degree, and Biola gave her a full-time position that she held for thirty-one years. I dropped back to doing just one job, teaching at Fuller.

CONTEXTUALIZATION

Returning to my work at Fuller, I'll start by referring to some of my writings. I have focused on four areas in my forty years as a missiologist: anthropology, communication, contextualization, and spiritual power. The books and articles I published were developed largely out of the courses I taught and provide an overview of my work.

Perhaps my most famous course and book was *Christianity in Culture*. From 1973 to 1979 I was able to work rather intensively on putting together my thoughts concerning the theological implications of the relationships between Christianity and culture. I began to develop the course soon after I arrived at Fuller, putting a number of my articles together to form the backbone of the course. I then applied for a sabbatical quarter in about 1975 or 1976 during which I would teach the course in a three-hour class once a week for ten weeks, promising the students drafts of two chapters a week of a new textbook for the course. So I worked hard in the little office in my garage to produce two chapters per week and kept my promise. The first draft of the manuscript of my book *Christianity in Culture* was developed in this way. Though there were three major revisions of the book before it was published in 1979, the basic approach was worked out with that class.

In this book I attempt to develop a cross-cultural approach to theologizing that I have called "Christian Ethnotheology." It is an early evangelical approach to contextualization, based on my own attempts to integrate what I had learned of theology and anthropology with what I had learned of how to deal with biblical data in a non-Western context. I suggested that we use the incarnation and informed Bible translation theory as developed largely by Eugene Nida as our models. My call was for churches, theologizing, conversion, and all other aspects of Christianity to be equivalent in meaning within contemporary societies to the approved models of these things we see in Scripture. I originally labeled this theory "dynamic equivalence" but now I prefer the label "meaning equivalence."

This resulted in very fruitful classroom interactions with our experienced student body and eventually in the publication of *Christianity in Culture* (1979). The book many consider to be my magnum opus. This book established me as a leader in the contextualization debates. It also made me quite controversial in some circles, though very affirmed in others and among our student body and School of Mission colleagues.

In some ways it is an angry book, developed out of the frustration of working under the mission practice of the day that I called an "extractionist" approach rather than Jesus' approach that I call "identificational" or "incarnational." The book got me widely criticized by what I call "closed conservatives" but praised by those seeking a post-colonial approach to mission that takes both the Bible and culture seriously.

In the later stages of the development of the book I made a pilgrimage to Bernard Ramm where he was on a church staff in Modesto, California. He had said in one of his books that when we learn more about language and culture, we may need to revise some of our theology. Since my book involved an approach to theologizing that I hoped incorporated a sharper knowledge of culture and language, I asked him if he thought my book was doing what he had called for. He sort of said yes and honored me by writing the foreword for the book.

Though published in 1979, *Christianity in Culture* was developed during most of the decade during which Evangelicals were debating the use of the word "contextualization." The term came in for widespread rejection by evangelicals due to the fact that it had been coined by Shoki Coe, a World Council scholar not trusted by Evangelicals. By the end of the decade, however, many were making their peace with the term.

I began to publish some of my thoughts on contextualization in the early seventies. Two articles in Fuller's *Theology, News and Notes* came out as early as 1972, entitled "Theology and Theologies I" and "II." These were followed in 1973 by "Toward a Christian Ethnotheology," in *God, Man and Church Growth*, in 1974 by "Christian Conversion as a Dynamic Process," and in 1976 by

"Cultural Concomittants of Higi Conversion: Early Period." These latter two zeroed in on a contextualized approach to conversion. I've reprinted them in the collection of many of my writings, entitled *Culture, Communication and Christianity* (William Carey, 2001).

Early in the '70s I was teaching a course called "Indigeneity," using the older term in order not to ruffle too many feathers. In 1973, I introduced the terms "ethnotheology" in "Toward a Christian Ethnotheology" (1973) and "dynamic equivalence" in "Dynamic Equivalence Churches" (1973) to avoid the term contextualization. Then, even as late as 1979 when Tom Wisley and I published a reader that now would be called a reader in contextualization, we chose to name it *Readings in Dynamic Indigeneity* (1979).

The influence I had in the landmark Willowbank Consultation (1978) spun off from my work on *Christianity in Culture* even though the conference came before the 1979 publication. Besides the presentation of my ideas, published as "The Church in Culture—A Dynamic Equivalence Model" (1978), the late Harvie Conn, a theologian, did a paper on conversion, using a prepublication version of my chapter on conversion in *Christianity in Culture* as the basis for his approach. In fact, as came out later in Conn's Church Growth Lectures (1983; published as *Eternal Word, Changing Worlds*, 1984) he went a long way toward educating himself in anthropology in order to understand what we were saying about contextualization. I could have asked no more from him or anyone else. He honored me, both at Willowbank and in the Church Growth Lectures. As a humorous aside, during those lectures he gave several possible titles to his presentations. One of these titles was "Did Charles Kraft Come from Heaven or from the Other Place?"

In several articles (*Culture, Communication of Chritianity*, Kraft 2001) and *Readings in Dynamic Indigeneity* (edited with Tom Wisley), I was able to further develop my approach to contextualization and to point to the importance of seeing indigenizing/ contextualizing as a dynamic process, regardless of whether we labeled it "indigenization" or "contextualization." Though some were contending that the term "contextualization" implied a more dynamic Christianity than "indigenization," I argued that our major concern should not be over the label, but over whether the approach to Christian faith was dynamic or static. So, I argued, those who used the older term but saw our faith as dynamic were on the right side while those who used the newer term but had a static view had not gotten the point.

My involvement in the study of the relationship between Christianity and culture produced a tension between Dean Mc-Gavran and myself. McGavran, with all his many gifts, seemed to me to have a fairly naïve attitude toward culture. He was fond of speaking of "Christian culture" as the practices of those who have become Christian in a given society. He even went so far as to define the term as an appropriate label for a society in which the majority of its people are Christians. My position was that, though people can be Christian, cultural structures cannot be. Thus, you can have a "Christian society," a "Christian people group," but not Christian structures. And culture is a term for structure, not people (see Kraft 1996, 2009). McGavran's overall position, stemming no doubt from his experiences in India, was that Christianity is against culture and though cultural phenomena can be used as bridges to Christianity or "Christian culture," he believed, Christian customs will inevitably replace traditional customs. McGavran could speak of Christian customs and non-Christian customs, as if certain practices are restricted to Christians and certain to non-Christians. My contention is that customs and cultures should not be so labeled, since all customs are structural, available for use by both Christians and non-Christians.

CHAPTER 10

THE BUSY MISSIOLOGIST

1974 MARSEILLES

IN 1974 I WAS invited to attend a conference sponsored by North Africa Mission in Marseilles, France, on communicating to Muslims. When I was invited by a communications professor in the Wheaton College Graduate School, I mentioned that I would probably create controversy because of my culture-friendly approach in a conference sponsored by such a conservative mission. He replied that that was the very reason he was inviting me. They assigned me several strange topics: "Distinctive Religious Barriers to Outside Penetration," "Extent and Limitations of Media among Muslims," and "Guidelines for Developing a Message Geared to the Horizon of Receptivity" were some of the titles. Among other things, I suggested (rightly or wrongly) that Islam looks very much like a contextualization of Muhammad's understanding of Christianity. This was taken very badly by some of the conservative participants. My lectures were published in *Media in Islamic Culture*, ed. C. Richard Shumaker (Wheaton, IL: International Christian Broadcasters, 1974).

1978: THE YEAR OF THE MUSLIM

The year 1978 was important for contextualization studies. Early in the year, a number of us participated in a conference held in Bermuda (we call it Willowbank in hopes nobody would find out that we were actually in Bermuda!). This was a serious attempt by the Lausanne Committee for World Evangelization to get theologians and anthropologists to sit down together to hammer out some of the issues in the relationships between theology, culture, and contextualization. In those meetings, evangelical theologians and anthropologists met for perhaps the first time ever to discuss missiological issues. I was seated between James Packer and Stephen Neil, perhaps to keep me from getting too far out of hand!

Besides Packer and Neil, theologians Harvie Conn, I. Howard Marshall, and Orlando Costas represented the theological side of things. On the anthropological side were Alan Tippett, Jake Loewen, Al Krass, Charles Taber, and myself. Under the masterful guidance of John Stott, we, anthropologists, and they, theologians, came to new appreciation of each other. Our papers were published in *Down to Earth: Studies in Christianity and Culture*, ed. John Stott and Robert Coote (Grand Rapids: Eerdmans 1980). I felt especially honored by Harvie Conn, who was assigned to deal with conversion and virtually spoke from my chapter on conversion in the manuscript of *Christianity in Culture*. He and others gave my concept of dynamically equivalent churches (and DE conversion) a pretty good airing.

Then, still in 1978, a whole issue of *Evangelical Missions Quarterly* was devoted to the subject of contextualization. There were articles by James Buswell, Ross Kinsler, and others. My article was entitled "The Contextualization of Theology." After this issue of *EMQ* and the Willowbank Conference, evangelical opposition to the word contextualization seems to have evaporated. I also did an article, published in the *Journal of the Evangelical Theological Society*, entitled "Interpreting in Cultural Context" (1978) that contributed to this important year's worth of contextualization studies.

Another significant thing that happened in 1978 was that we declared it "The Year of the Muslim" at SWM. We had been challenged to deal with this large block of resistant people and felt that some of the new experiments to win them should be taught, examined, and discussed. Don McCurry, who was studying with us at Fuller at the time, was given an adjunct position and given courses to teach on winning Muslims. We also brought in the late Ken Bailey to teach at SWM . He was a scholar of Islam who lived for years in the Middle East. Each of us who had done something toward winning Muslims, or theorized concerning how to win them, focused on Muslims in our classes.

Still another event in 1978 was the Pan African Christian Leadership Assembly (PACLA) in Nairobi. My papers were titled: "Christianity and Culture in Africa," "What Is an Indigenous Church?" and "Strategies for Reaching Africa's 300 Million Lost." The papers from that assembly were published by Evangel Publishing House in *Facing the New Challenges—the Message of PACLA* (Nairobi: Evangel, 1978).

Another event at this conference centered on my presentations. One of my plenary presentations involved an evaluation of John Mbiti's approach to Christianity in Africa and it's relationship to a conflict between Mbiti and Byang Kato, who had recently died. A sizeable group of evangelicals at the conference were expecting me to come down hard on Mbiti in favor of what I considered an unfair attack by Kato on Mbiti in Kato's book *Theological Pitfalls in Africa* and in other places. Mbiti had a reputation as a World Council liberal and one can find much to criticize in his writings. But he took what I considered a reasonable position on contextualization in Africa in his paper for the conference.

I did two things that angered these Evangelicals, especially a group of very conservative leaders from Nigeria. I spoke positively of Mbiti's position and I announced in a plenary session that Kato had been Christian enough to apologize to Mbiti for some of the unkind (and, I believe, unprofessional) things he had said about him and his position. This announcement earned me a visit from the Nigerians who tried to get me to retract my announcement!

This I considered absurd. How does one retract an announcement? I'm not sure what the fallout of this event was, but probably I lost my position as an evangelical in the minds of the Nigerians and perhaps others.

ANTHROPOLOGY

An early recognition of my focus on anthropology in relation to theology came with an invitation to write a longish paper to be presented to the Board of the *Christian Scholars Review* and then published in their journal. My thirty-seven-page paper was entitled "Can Anthropological Insight Assist Evangelical Theology?" The cool reception by that group underlined for me the fact that people without cross-cultural experience are severely hampered in evaluating an approach to the Bible and theology that takes seriously God's working within (rather than against) culture.

The anthropology courses I taught at Fuller eventually led to the publication of one of my major books, *Anthropology for Christian Witness* (Orbis, 1996). In that book I attempt to teach what we had practiced in Nigeria—a culture-friendly approach based on Christian presuppositions. I used anthropology as a perspective more than simply a subject, helping people to see "through anthropological eyes." With our student body of mostly experienced people, there were many whose ministries were changed through the anthropology course.

COMMUNICATION

I, following Nida, helped bring a focus on communication theory into church growth missiology both in the communication classes I taught and in several of my books. My main course in this area was the Intercultural Communication course out of which came *Communication Theory for Christian Witness* (rev. ed., Orbis, 1991) and *Communicating Jesus' Way* (William Carey, 1979, 1999).

The book now titled *Communicating Jesus' Way* was developed from lectures I gave at Ashland Seminary in 1979. Ashland published the lectures in their Ashland *Theological Bulletin* (1979) and later I was able to take these lectures and come out with a more formally published book entitled *Communicating the Gospel God's Way*. William Carey Library published it. I later expanded it and in 1999 William Carey published a new revised and enlarged edition named *Communicating Jesus' Way*. I was pleased by the comment of a specialist in communication who was at that time working in Nairobi. She said something like, "This is the only communication book I know of that really communicates!"

AICC

As I developed my approach to intercultural communication, we attracted students who wanted to focus on communication. Among the students we attracted were two outstanding Scandanavians, Knud Jorgensen from Norway and Viggo Sogaard from Denmark. Both of these men had been working as missionaries and as communication specialists—Knud in Ethiopia and Viggo in Thailand. They came to SWM at about the same time in the early '80s.

Viggo had been studying at Wheaton under Jim Engel at the MA level and, at Engel's recommendation, applied to SWM to continue his studies to doctoral level under me. I had heard about this and recommended to Dean Pierson that he get acquainted with Viggo at the Lausanne 1980 meeting in Patayya, Thailand. Viggo had a hand in planning that conference and made more than one plenary presentation. I asked Pierson to invite Viggo to come study with us and also to do some teaching in the area of communication. This he did and I was assigned to be Viggo's PhD mentor. This started a very fine friendship between Viggo and myself (and between Ketty, his wife, and Meg).

One of the projects Viggo invested himself in was the Asian Institute for Christian Communication, a training program for Asian communicators. It was started in 1979 as a five-week course to which organizations such as World Vision, United Bible Societies, Far Eastern Broadcasting Corporation, and others sent their personnel to receive instruction in communication theory and practice. This institute has now been discontinued (after thirteen summer sessions) but when it was in operation we met every two or three years in Chiang Mai, Thailand. Meg and I have been on the faculty for eleven of the thirteen sessions.

The students did the classes, readings, and a term project that received Fuller credit for those enrolled at SWM. We usually attracted thirty to forty students and have been able to influence a number of those who were working in print and radio communication throughout Asia.

CHAPTER 11

CHRISTIANITY WITH POWER

MY EVANGELICAL BACKGROUND

AS MENTIONED, THE CHURCH I grew up in was a solid evangelical church. By "evangelical" I mean solidly biblical but not charismatic. The church was made up of people who had become fed up with the theological liberalism of the other churches in our area. So, the members were very Bible-centered and had the conviction that they had "come out from among them," separating themselves from people they considered apostate or at least ignorant of true Christianity. They/I felt we had the truth and that God was on our side.

I took these attitudes to Christian camp, then to Wheaton, then to Ashland Seminary, then to Nigeria, then to Hartford, and on to Fuller. I had broadened quite a bit by seminary days and in working in an American Baptist church in Hartford but still was solidly evangelical (and non-charismatic) in my posture.

While still at Fuller in 1982 a very surprising thing happened to me. Ever since my years in Nigeria, I had been puzzled about the relevance of Jesus' teaching and behavior relating to healing, demons, and other manifestations of spiritual power. I had asked the Nigerian church leaders what their biggest problem was and they had said, without hesitation, "evil spirits." They asked me what they should do about them, and, though I took both their questions and the existence of demons seriously, I had no answers for them.

However, my understanding of what is going on in the world in response to gospel witness was growing as I participated in and helped shape Church Growth Missiology. I had my own experience with missionary Christianity, of course, and had plenty to say about that. I knew from comparing notes with our missionary students at Fuller that the kind of churches my Mission had been planting were quite typical of many missionary churches—powerless and largely secular.

I taught against that kind of church, advocating a culture-friendly approach. As I taught and discussed and read, however, I became increasingly aware of the fact that there were other churches, quite unlike the kind my mission had established. There were what we used to call "African Independent (or African Initiative) Churches," usually more in tune with African culture and emotion. And there were the Pentecostals—known for healing and emotion. Neither of these kinds of Christianity were in our focus as we worked in Nigeria. But reports of students at SWM made it clear to me that these kinds of churches were often experiencing greater growth than those of my kind of evangelicalism.

And there were churches that had answers that I didn't have to the question the Nigerians had asked me, "What do we do about evil spirits?"

I was becoming increasingly aware of the fact that, beyond the multitude of problems relating to culture and colonialism, worldwide missionary Christianity was lacking the spiritual power we are promised in the New Testament. I didn't know what to do about this except to identify it as best I could and move on. I did, rather unconsciously, make a prophetic statement in 1979 in *Christianity in Culture* (239–40) about the need for missionaries to Africa to be able to pray effectively for healing. I have no idea where that came from, since I had no experience in this area.

At this point a nearby Pentecostal seminary fell apart and we at Fuller attracted many of their students. Furthermore, I was discovering that many of our missionary and international students were coming from a Pentecostal or charismatic background. This made a problem for me since these students kept asking the question: "Where is the Holy Spirit?" in what I was recommending to them. And I didn't know.

I believe I was doing well in helping my students to understand the cultural and communicational aspects of Christian witness cross-culturally. But I had no understanding of where the power of the Holy Spirit fit in. So I began searching. I started to get to know some of the charismatics, especially an Australian Pentecostal named Kevin Hovey and his wife, Glenys. They helped me greatly to change some of my stereotypes of what Pentecostals and charismatics were all about. I had expected highly emotional persons of questionable intelligence. What I found was highly intelligent, deeply spiritual, and highly committed persons, thoroughly likeable and very helpful in every way. I wonder if they knew I was studying them! We got to be fast friends.

MOVING INTO POWER MINISTRY

In addition, Meg and I began visiting John Wimber's church on Sunday evenings. Wimber had been working with Peter Wagner doing church growth studies and teaching under the auspices of Fuller Evangelistic Association. After a couple of years of this, Wimber resigned from FEA to develop his wife's Bible study group into a church that would be committed to a healing ministry. By 1981, this church had grown to attracting about two thousand attendees Sunday mornings and another two thousand in the evening with some fascinating things going on there—healings and deliverances as well as solid evangelicalism.

In 1981, then, Wagner brought a proposal to an SWM faculty meeting that we invite Wimber to teach a course on healing. As we discussed this, we recognized that Wimber's ministry was to Americans, not cross-cultural. So we decided to offer him and his course to the School of Theology. They refused the course, so we discussed it again and decided to do it ourselves with Wagner the "professor of record" (= in charge) and Wimber doing the teaching. It would be Wagner's course. He would be the one in charge and he would deal with the assignments and assign the grades. We decided that we'd offer the course in Winter Term, starting in January of 1982, meeting on Monday evenings from 7 to 10.

Eighty-five students enrolled in the course. Peter and Doris Wagner and Meg and I also attended. And God used that course to change our lives. With three major questions in my mind, I was an enthusiastic supporter of the course from the beginning. The first question was the one I could not answer in Nigeria: "What do we do about evil spirits?" The second was the one the students were asking: "Where is the Holy Spirit?" In addition, I remembered a question I had had for a long time: "Isn't there more to Christianity than this?" (my evangelical, non charismatic version of the faith).

The fact that we had known Wimber as a researcher and a "regular guy" helped a lot in giving credibility to what he taught. He was not a "raving Pentecostal." But when he taught, he taught as a practitioner who knew and followed the Scriptures. And when he spoke healing, it usually happened. He brought with him a team of gifted healers and we would see as many as ten to fifteen healings every session. He'd teach for two of the three hours and then close his book, saying, "Now it's time to do the stuff." He'd ask the Holy Spirit to come and we'd wait for the first person to speak a "word of knowledge," to let us know who the Holy Spirit wanted to heal. Usually John or one of his team would speak the first "word," then others would speak what they had heard from the Holy Spirit.

One of these that sticks in my mind is when one of the team received a "word" and said something like, "There's someone here with a back problem, wearing a brace with something shiny in it." A young lady raised her hand, suggesting that the shiny thing was a grommet in the back brace. John spoke healing to the condition and it was healed.

On another occasion, John said that there was someone in the audience with a bad headache. He said something like, "It started at about four this afternoon and feels like someone has driven a spike into your head. It's the strangest headache you have ever had. It feels like it's going round and round your head. Who is it?" A lady raised her hand and described her headache just as John had said. It was soon healed.

There was a steady stream of such words of knowledge each evening and God usually healed whoever responded to the words. It was like New Testament times again! And we all became believers in a new way. I guess I did believe that God healed directly on occasion. But the healings we had heard about were usually thousands of miles away, making it easy to believe that God healed directly only in faraway places but used doctors and medicine here at home. But now in a seminary classroom here at home, God was healing people with whom we could interact the next day or the next week. New Testament stuff was actually happening right in our classroom!

This first offering of the course, from January to March of 1982, brought about incredible change in my life. For the first time, I was able to see firsthand how the Holy Spirit can work in power for healing, for deliverance from demons, and for any number of other blessings, and all in a matter-of-fact, non-weird way. Wimber became for me and many of the rest of our students a credible witness to the fact that Christianity is not intended to be powerless.

I remembered a time in Nigeria when the village shaman began to come to church. He had been impressed by the fact that our school headmaster had dismissed school and brought about ninety school children to the funeral of his wife. His comment was, "I never knew you Christians cared about me and my family." He was a polygamist and felt rejected by the church but the love he experienced made him curious. He started attending church. But, after a few weeks he dropped away, probably because there was no power in the church. The preacher talked a lot about a miracle-worker who lived long ago and did wonderful things. But neither the pastor nor any of the other Christians could do those things now. In fact, when they (including the Nigerian preacher) needed power, they came to him (the shaman) rather than going to Jesus or the pastor. As I reflected on our time in Nigeria, I began to see that the biggest lack in our ministry was not the lack of cultural appropriateness, as I had been teaching. It was the lack of spiritual power.

Indeed, the biggest problem in worldwide Christianity is the lack of spiritual power because most of the peoples of the world are power oriented and we are offering them powerless Christianity. And the churches that were growing were usually (not always) Pentecostal or charismatic—churches that believed in and practiced healing and deliverance. In the discussions leading up to inviting Wimber to teach us on healing, I saw vaguely the need for our students to learn what Wimber could teach us. This conviction deepened, then, as the class went on and we learned what Wimber was teaching—how to work in partnership with God to heal, deliver, and bless. And I determined that my students would not go away from my classes as ignorant in this area as I had gone to Nigeria.

So I listened as Wimber taught. And watched as he and his team members ministered in power. He encouraged us to start ministering healing. I began rather tentatively, taking authority over physical problems and saw some healing but many disappointments.

Early in our experience with Holy Spirit-guided healing we discovered that praying for (or, rather, commanding) physical healing as Wimber had taught us wasn't always effective. Often nothing would happen—we found that only about a third of those we prayed for got completely healed. Or, the person would get well immediately but the condition would return in a day or two. This alerted me to the fact that people often need a deeper healing experience if they are to get completely well. Learning this nudged me toward dealing with emotional and spiritual problems, a focus that was called "inner healing." In addition we noticed that when people received ministry for inner healing, physical problems often went away totally when prayed for at the end of the inner healing session.

INNER HEALING

My conversion to inner healing from just praying for physical healing as Wimber had taught us to do happened one evening at the Anaheim Vineyard in about 1983. The worship and preaching was over and people had gathered in small groups to pray for those who requested it.

I and a couple of others began praying for a rather large man who told us he had a very sore ankle. We prayed for the physical problem and nothing happened. Then what came into my mind was something I had heard long ago—that most physical problems have emotional roots. So I asked the fellow two questions: "When did the pain start?" and "What else was going on in your life when the pain started?" The man then told us he had had a motorcycle accident that hurt the ankle but that it had healed.

However, about a month ago, the ankle had begun hurting again soon after he had recommitted his life to Christ. He told us that he had once been very close to Jesus but had allowed himself to drift away, remaining backslidden for the better part of two years. A month ago, however, he had come under conviction and returned to Christ. That's when the ankle began to hurt again. I asked him if he was feeling guilty about his backsliding. He answered that he was feeling very guilty. He wondered just how he who had had a close walk with Jesus could have turned away from him and stayed away so long.

So we dealt with his guilt and the forgiveness that Jesus gives us if we give him our guilt and shame and forgive ourselves. As we prayed through these issues, then, and he finally was able to forgive himself, he looked up and said, "It doesn't hurt anymore!" His real problem was not the ankle, but the guilt and his inability to forgive himself. When those issues were taken care of, his system was able to release him from the pain of the ankle injury.

This event taught me something important. That is, that physical healing can be hindered by emotional problems but healing can come if the emotional problems are taken care of. What I was learning was that digging deeper than the surface-level physical problems was often the way to bring healing to those who did not respond to our prayers for physical healing. This and several subsequent similar experiences, then, were leading me to discover that my gifting lies more for healing in the emotional and spiritual area than for physical healing. This was the start of my commitment to inner healing. From this point on, I seldom pray for a physical problem without also dealing with the deeper emotions of a person.

I learned another lesson as well. Wimber had taught us that obedience precedes gifting. Many people wait to find out what their gifts are before they risk praying for healing. They feel that gifting comes first, then they can minister. But I firmly believe that we are to launch out to find out how God has gifted us in the process of ministering. I believe this is what happened in my life. I began praying for the physically hurting and before long discovered that my area of gifting is in dealing with emotional and spiritual problems. In my ministry I see many people healed of physical problems but few of them are healed without receiving emotional or spiritual healing first.

SPIRITUAL POWER IN MISSIOLOGY

The incorporation of a focus on spiritual power in my missiology came as a result of the fact that I saw very little focus on this area in missiology or in mission practice. I felt that healing and deliverance, so important in Jesus' life and ministry, were being neglected both in the classroom and in the field. So I determined that I would try to fill the vacuum as best I could, teaching and practicing a Christianity with power.

This change in my missiology has brought gratifying response in some quarters and criticism from others. Some seem to want to continue a powerless Christianity—a Christianity that may acknowledge that Jesus healed and dealt with demons but ignores the fact that he passed these forms of ministry on. Theirs is what I call "Powerless Christianity."

My first book in this area was *Christianity with Power* (1989), where I applied worldview theory to the paradigm shift we Evangelicals have to go through to move into this dimension of biblical Christianity. Wagner considered this book a major contributor to the process of paradigm shifting going on with many Evangelicals. My *Evangelical Missions Quarterly* article "What Kind of Encounters Do We Need?" (1991) was one of my next publications (see below), where I seek a balanced faith that involves three kinds of encounters: Allegiance leading to Relationship, Truth leading to Understanding, and Power leading to Freedom.

THE THREE ENCOUNTERS

One of my next major contributions to the importance of dealing with spiritual power in missiology was two chapters in my contextualization books *Appropriate Christianity* (2002) and *Issues in Contextualization* (2016). The titles of these chapters are "Spiritual Power: A Missiological Issue" and "Appropriate Contextualization of Spiritual Power." A further chapter in that book is a more developed presentation of the three encounters concept. A complete Christianity is experienced as a relationship with Jesus, entered into by pledging allegiance to him in that relationship. A Christian relationship, then, is to be supported by a focus on truth/ knowledge leading to understanding, plus a parallel experience of spiritual power leading to freedom. Evangelicals have focused primarily on the truth dimension and on relationship, but often neglected the power dimension.

Though the power of God to heal and deliver from demons is prominent in the Gospels, most of Evangelical Christianity has ignored the fact that both in the NT and in contemporary life, especially in the non-Western world, the exercise of spiritual power is a major concern. But most missionary activity presents a rather secularized faith, ill suited to attract people who seek spiritual power.

This concept is summarized in the following diagram:

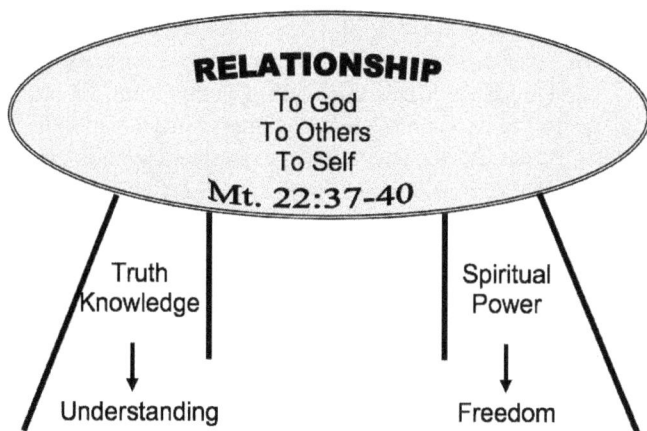

WRITING AND MINISTERING IN SPIRITUAL POWER

Following *Christianity with Power*, I have published twelve more semi-popular books on inner healing, deliverance, authority, and spiritual warfare. In addition, I began to minister to students and others, starting in about 1985 and to teach inner healing in weekend seminars throughout the United States and overseas.

To date, under the guidance of the Holy Spirit I have ministered one-on-one to hundreds of people, with amazing success in getting them free from internal emotional and spiritual problems. One of many testimonials that I've received is as follows:

> My life has been soooo great since you and God set me free!!!!! The rest of the day (Thurs.) there were praise songs or hymns playing in the back of my mind—and for 2 days all of my senses were heightened so that I felt like everything around me I was experiencing for the first time. Finally I can wake up looking forward to the day and actually plan for the future—without the feeling of dread. I don't feel double-minded, much more confident in the thoughts and feelings that I have. My addiction to caffeine keeps weakening each day—that is helping my headaches. I feel no anxiety or fears—what a new way

> to approach life!! And best of all I can actually feel the
> warmth of God's love—to really know in my heart that
> He loves me—not just in my mind!! It makes trusting
> God much easier now that I feel so close to Him. Thank
> you a thousand times for taking time to help me!!!!!!!!!!!!
> . . . I feel so sad that so many Protestant churches are
> denying spiritual oppression, therefore condemning be-
> lievers to a life of bondage—it's not fair!!!! Well, I want to
> continue to learn more (Sharon Batten, May 14, 1998).

For most Christians, freedom seems to be a step beyond
salvation (see Kraft 2002 for more on this subject). This lady had
been saved for several years but was not free. We are promised
newness (2 Cor 5:17) but for most of us, this is something we have
to work out in our Christian lives. Freedom doesn't seem to come
automatically for most people. But God has led me into inner healing as a way to lead people into that freedom.

The way I see it, there are three really big things in Christianity: salvation, of course, then freedom, followed by dealing with
the old habits and replacing them with new ones. The one of these
God has called me to focus on is the second: freedom and to some
extent dealing with the habits. Large numbers of Christians are
wonderfully saved but not free. Deep-level healing is a way to work
with Jesus to lead people to freedom in Christ so they can experience the freedom that has been promised to them in Scripture and
church. This is what the lady quoted above was experiencing.

TEACHING ON SPIRITUAL POWER AT FULLER

So, I became a practitioner, joining Jesus in "setting captives free"
(Luke 4:18–19). But, as mentioned above, there was also an academic part to this change in me. Moving into the area of spiritual
power has made a much more complete missiologist out of me as
well as a much more fulfilled servant of Jesus Christ. But, some
would say, a strange anthropologist and a strange academic!

Some say that I have left my first love, assuming that the real
me is the academic missiologist. I say to them, "Though I love

missiology, my first love is to follow Jesus in the ministry he gave his life for—showing God's love for people, using God's power to set them free from the enemy." I do this at two levels: first, in ministering the power of Jesus at the individual level and second, attempting to integrate my experience with God's power into my teaching. I am committed to a missiology with power.

Some call me an academic. I have paid my dues to academia. I now have published thirty-seven books and taught in several areas at graduate level in four institutions for nearly fifty years. But I would maintain that academics is something I do, not something I am. I do academic things but that is not where I live. I may be called a Christian, a missionary, a teacher, a linguist, an anthropologist, a missiologist, and, yes, an academic. But my commitment is to Jesus and to people. And I do academic things as well as ministry things to serve, not to define myself. I see myself as a servant of Christ who has learned a few things about how God works in this world. And I am ready not only to talk and write about those things but also to practice what he gave his life for: to set captives free (Luke 4:18–19).

By 1984 courses in spiritual power taught by Wimber were drawing much attention both inside and outside the seminary. Students were flocking to these courses and raising embarrassing questions in other classes concerning healing. The basic course was attracting close to three hundred students (the largest enrollment in any class at Fuller) and we had introduced a second level course. Opposition arose within the seminary leading to the cancelling of the courses in 1985.

But the students requested permission to offer the course as a student activity rather than as an academic course. I did a lecture on worldview, including a discussion of the changes that were taking place in my own thinking and behavior.

After one of the sessions, when we were doing ministry, a couple of ladies came up to me with a report that they were ministering to another lady and had hit something they couldn't handle. Assuming that I would know what to do, they came to me for help. What I found was a lady sitting stiffly on a chair, not responding to the ladies who were trying to help her. I took one look and said to myself something like, "Well, I knew it would happen sooner or later, I'm about to meet my first demon." I took charge, commanded the demon to obey us and got him out. And the group that was watching probably never knew that this was my first face-to-face encounter with a demon! In about half an hour we got the lady free from this and several other demons. And I got to experience the power of the Holy Spirit that has been given to us.

The course as a student activity did not satisfy Wagner and me. We applied to the provost to do an academic course, one that would not be taught by Wimber. Wagner and I would offer it and, we would agree to have lectures by both opponents and proponents of healing today. This we did for the next two years. We met once a week for ten weeks with a different lecturer each week. We had positive speakers (including Wimber) and negative speakers and had a thoroughly academic airing of views—a typical seminary course where everything got talked about and nothing much got done outside the classroom.

After we had done the course this way for two years, Wagner and I appealed to the provost to allow Peter to offer a course on physical healing while I developed one on inner healing. Wagner's course was accepted but mine was rejected. This bothered me, of course, until the provost suggested that I develop a course on power encounter. However, he had heard that my former senior colleague, Alan Tippett, had used the term power encounter in an academic context and so he indicated that if I developed such a course, he would approve it.

I began teaching the Power Encounter course in the 1989–90 year and was able to introduce the Deep Healing course (my name for inner healing) within a year or two after that. Wagner developed a couple of other spiritual power courses before he left us in 1996. I took over his Confronting the Powers course (dealing with cosmic-level spiritual activity) and taught three courses one each term from then on: Deep Healing, Power Encounter, and Confronting the Powers.

CHAPTER 12

SENT TO THE WORLD

INTERCULTURAL RENEWAL / DEEP HEALING MINISTRIES

ONE DAY IN 1987 I received a phone call from an Australian student of ours asking me to come to Orange County (south of Los Angeles) to sign some papers. My reaction was, "Do what?" He explained that he and another student had met with a lawyer and needed me to formalize the start of a new organization to do inner healing ministry. My reaction was to say, "But that will cost money, won't it?" "Yes," he replied, "but we can find the money." And they did.

The three of us had for several months been batting around the idea of an organization to sponsor inner healing seminars and training sessions for missionaries in the field since most had no training in this area. But I wasn't in on any plan to actually sign us up. The students though, had gotten impatient and gone ahead and researched what needed to be done and then done it. All they needed was my signature as president of the new entity.

So I dutifully met them, signed the papers, and "Intercultural Renewal Ministries" was born. I've forgotten how we arrived at that name but it pointed to a major aim of ours—to do something that would assist missionaries both with their personal problems and with their ability to minister to people who are power oriented. We anticipated doing seminars both in the United States and abroad to help those in ministry to be more effective. The students would take care of the administrative end of things and I would teach.

So IRM was born. I collected teaching materials developed by Wimber's associates plus books and pamphlets from other sources to develop seminars on inner healing and deliverance. These materials, combined with my own stuff developed for the Power Encounter and Deep Healing courses at Fuller provided teaching materials for our seminars.

As mentioned before, I also had published *Christianity with Power* (1989) with an evangelical audience in mind. The aim was in line with the seminars we were doing—to move evangelicals into spiritual power. We were getting invitations from various evangelical churches to do weekend seminars that we named "Love and Power Seminars." In these, I taught on spiritual power, inner healing, and deliverance. We also demonstrated inner healing ministry by choosing a person to minister to with the attendees looking on. From the beginning we wanted people to observe the ministry as well as to hear about it.

CYPRUS AND ISRAEL

Before long, we got our first invitation to bring a team to teach and demonstrate overseas. Our first engagement was to Cyprus and Israel. In Cyprus a very special thing happened as we were ministering to the pastor's wife. She had suffered for thirty years with a severe back problem. We prayed for the problem as a physical problem but nothing happened. Then we got into her inner feelings and found that she had been absorbing all of the problems of her husband's pastorate—animosity toward him, gossip, backbiting—all the typical stuff that a pastor has to put up with. When she was able to give all that stuff to Jesus and to forgive the perpetrators, her back got well instantly! And she never had another problem with her back till her death about ten years later. In fact, she wrote me about an experience she had in Rome when she fell down a flight of stairs. Fearing her back problem would come back, she got up very carefully. But no pain. No problem!

We ministered in an Anglican church in Tel Aviv, Israel. I had an important experience on the plane coming home. The night before we left, we had been fighting with a strong demon for several hours but never got him out. I remember sitting on the plane complaining to the Lord that he had allowed the demon to remain, even though the lady badly wanted to get free. As I complained, though, I heard the Lord say to me, "Well, at least this time you were trying!" And I was led to reflect on many years of ministry when I didn't know how to get people free and didn't even try. We heard a couple of years later that someone had been able to free her. Praise the Lord.

MOROCCO

One of our next trips was to Morocco in about 1995. We were invited to do a seminar for a handful of missionaries. We met in a very small Anglican church in Casa Blanca and stayed in a nearby hotel. The church was so small that when we divided up for ministry, some of us had to minister outside in the graveyard that surrounded the church. One of our team members called the cemetery "the bone yard"!

I was asked to preach in that little church on Sunday. It had a high pulpit that required several stairs steps to get up to. I at first said to myself, "There's no way that I'll preach from that pulpit." But then it occurred to me that I could use that pulpit to demonstrate an important point about the incarnation. So, I started my sermon up in the pulpit and spoke of a God who is majestic and awesome, high above the world and its ills. But, I continued, this is not the whole picture of our God. For, I said as I came down the pulpit stairs, the most impressive thing about God is that he came down and became one of us, taking on our flesh and living as one of us. I then spoke of the incarnation as God's greatest miracle. I thought it was a pretty good sermon. The British consulate thought so too. He was sitting in the second row, right in front of me as I spoke. He shook my hand and said something like, "That's the most impressive sermon I've ever heard." I felt good about it.

There were a number of miraculous things that took place among the missionaries. One of them came during our ministry to a missionary wife who had been in deep depression for almost a year and was on the verge of being sent home. We worked with her through a number of issues, many stemming from the fact that she as the oldest girl in her family had been given adult responsibility from age nine and, in effect, missed her childhood. As we worked through that, helping her to forgive and kicking the demons out, she got marvelously free. And God gave her a meaningful picture of herself in a letter jacket running with Jesus on a football field with the crowd cheering. I asked her if Jesus noticed the crowd. Her reply was something like, "No . . . He only has eyes for me." And she was freed and is free to this day to serve as a missionary to Muslims.

A side story to this was that years later I was asked to minister to her daughter, who was attending university and had tried for five years to get rid of a serious headache. She had sought help from professionals, but to no avail. God used us to set her free from the headaches, from a number of other problems that bound her, and from the demons that had attached themselves to her.

MORE SEMINARS

Soon we were invited to do seminars in Jos, Nigeria, Taiwan, and Switzerland. Over the years we've done seminars in Canberra, Brisbane, Melbourne, Perth, and Adelaide in Australia. One year I was able to participate in the Wimber meetings in Canberra and in Auckland, New Zealand. I had the opportunity to offer seminars and teach on spiritual power at the Bible College of New Zealand.

I was privileged to minister in Hong Kong with Jackie Pullinger Tan, who had been ministering to drug addicts in the Walled City since 1963. In addition to her significant work with the addicts, she was anxious for Hong Kong churches to be open to power ministry. She judged, however, that Wimber's approach might be too much for Hong Kong at first but that my approach might be more acceptable for a start. So she invited me to come twice to minister to her former addicts and also to participate in a mini seminar for church people to open them up to healing.

In 1995, our team was invited by a Swiss ministry of Campus Crusade named Koinonia to do a seminar in Switzerland. I remember my first impression of the Swiss audience with their mental arms crossed, daring us to break through their resistance. But then I did a public ministry session with one of them and that changed the whole atmosphere. They saw one of their own get healed. We were invited back year after year for seventeen years. At first, we took four or five team members to lead the demonstrations we did. People would sign up for ministry and the team members would each lead a group, ministering to the volunteer. Before long, some of the Swiss began doing the ministry. So I took fewer team members and we increased the number of ministry times with some of the Swiss leading, in German rather than through translation. Though we no longer go, the ministry continues. Little did I ever think God would give me opportunity to teach and minister in so many places. Besides those already mentioned we have served in Korea, Norway, Japan, India, Spain, Holland, Kenya, and Thailand.

CHAPTER 13

AFRICAN LANGUAGE
SPECIALIST: 1960–1970

IN ACADEMIC LIFE, ESPECIALLY at the graduate level at which I functioned for all of my career, a scholar is known largely by the things he/she publishes. My story would be incomplete, then, if I did not provide a tour through nearly fifty years of publications.

MY DISSERTATION

The senior linguist at Hartford, Henry Alan (Al) Gleason had started to publish the doctoral theses on linguistics produced by students in the Kennedy School of Missions. Indeed, he had us submit our dissertations on mimeograph stencils so they could be run off in quantity. I've forgotten how many copies he had made of each dissertation, but one would be submitted for the degree and anybody interested could buy our theses as volumes in the series he called *Hartford Studies in Linguistics*. My dissertation was "A Study of Hausa Syntax" (1963) in 3 volumes—volumes 8, 9, and 10 of that series (717 pp.).

The way the dissertation got to be three volumes is worthy of comment. The dissertation was really only volume one. A study of

Hausa syntax had been agreed on as my PhD dissertation. But as I went along, my collection of Hausa phrases, clauses, and sentences generated a rather impressive file of function words (i.e., prepositions, conjunctions, and other "small words"). I mentioned this to Dr. Gleason and asked what I should do with it. He said, "Write it up." This became the second volume of the book. The texts I worked from made up the third volume.

FINISHING UP MY HAUSA CAREER

Between 1964 and 1973 I pretty well finished my career as an African language specialist. In 1964 I introduced my dissertation to the scholarly world in an article entitled "A New Study of Hausa Syntax" (*Journal of African Languages*, 3:66–74). Those few people "into" an understanding either of Hausa structure or of comparative language syntax should find it useful. The study impressed my professors enough for them to grant me the PhD.

To further solidify my claim to be regarded as a scholar, a linguist, and a Hausa specialist, I did a series of fairly technical articles: "The Morpheme na in Relation to a Broader Classification of Hausa Verbals," *Journal of African Languages* (1964) 3:231–40; "Hausa sai and da—a Couple of Overworked Particles," *JA.L* (1970) 9:92–109, and "A Note on Lateral Fricatives in Chadic," *Studies in African Linguistics* (1971) 2:271–81.

In 1965 from Michigan State I began publishing teaching materials on Hausa. I had been working on these since our time in Nigeria and using them in my teaching at Michigan State. I imitated what Al Gleason had done at Hartford and developed an informally published series of *African Language Monographs* at Michigan State. Numbers 5A and B were my *An Introduction to Spoken Hausa* (textbook, workbook, tapes). These were labeled *African Language Monographs* 5A, 5B. (African Studies Center: Michigan State University, 1965). Then in 1966 I added volumes 6A and B to that series. Volume 6A was entitled *Cultural Materials in Hausa*, African Language Monograph 6A (African Studies Center: Michigan State University, 1966); 6B was a *Workbook in*

Intermediate and Advanced Hausa, African Language Monograph 6B (African Studies Center: Michigan State University, 1966).

Two of these MSU publications were formalized in 1973 and published by University of California Press as *Introductory Hausa*, with M. G. Kraft, and *A Hausa Reader*. I also was able to publish *Teach Yourself Hausa*, with A. H. M. Kirk-Greene (English Universities Press, 1973). This was a book that Tony Kirk-Greene was working on when we were teaching a Hausa course at Syracuse University in the summer of 1963. What he was putting together was what we call a "Reference Grammar" as opposed to a "Pedagogical Grammar." As we taught from it, Tony became aware of the fact that my command of the grammar was greater than his, so he gave the book to me. He recommended that I be the only author but the British publisher, rightly recognizing that Tony would be better known than I in England, insisted that both our names be on the book, even though it really had become my book rather than his as I revised it. I worked hard on the book and it came out quite well. Toni, from England, had lived in Northern Nigeria as a government officer for several years and was very fluent in Hausa. However, when we were at a party together with a group of Northern Nigerians, they embarrassed me by discussing whether Tony's or my Hausa was better. This in spite of the fact that I had not lived there for nearly as long as he had and did not have nearly the vocabulary he had. I think, though, that their evaluation was made on my command of the tones of the language rather than on fluency. Tony would frequently mispronounce the words tonally.

To wrap up my involvement in Hausa and African linguistics, I did four additional articles and a book:

1. One was a little language-learning booklet that Meg and I did together for Peace Corps entitled *Where Do I Go from Here?* (US Peace Corps, 1966). This is a handbook to help Peace Corps people continue their language learning on the field.

2. Then I did a more technical article based on a presentation at a conference for a volume edited by a former UCLA student, entitled "Reconstructions of Chadic Pronouns I: Possessive,

Object, and Independent Sets—An Interim Report," in *Third Annual Conference on African Linguistics*, ed. Erhard Voeltz (Indiana University Publications: African Series, 1974), 7:69–94.

3. I did a fun article on Hausa riddling that was published both in Nigeria and in Poland, entitled "Toward an Ethnography of Hausa Riddling," *Ba Shiru* 6 (1975) 171–24, and *Folia Orientalia* (Krakow, Poland) 17 (1976) 231–43. Frequently in Africa, riddling functions as a teaching device, a kind of catechism, by means of which children learn the worldview of the society.

4. This was followed by another fun article on Hausa epithets (witty labels given to persons and things). This was published in a festschrift for my colleague and mentor Bill Welmers, entitled "An Ethnolinguistic Study of Hausa Epithets," *Studies in African Linguistics*, Supplement 6: Papers in African Linguistics in Honor of Wm. E. Welmers, Department of Linguistics, University of California, Los Angeles (1976) 135–46. An epithet is a kind of nickname or pithy description of something that is useful in educating children or in word play. An example would be, "Igbo, slave of yams," meaning Igbos love to eat yams.

5. My final contribution to African linguistics, then, didn't get published till 1981, though it was completed earlier. It was a three-volume collection of word lists in sixty-five different languages, most of them related to Hausa, that I had collected during my 1966–67 year of research in Nigeria, entitled simply *Chadic Wordlists*, 3 vols. (Berlin: Verlag von Dietrich Reimer, 1981). Fuller came up with the $10,000 that the publisher required in order to put these wordlists in print. Though only those working on Nigerian languages would be interested in these lists and the tentative phonology for each language that I and some UCLA students had worked out, a lot of work went into these volumes.

By 1972 it was obvious that my career in missiology was where my future lay and that my career in linguistics was coming to an end, especially in a place such as UCLA where they taught a theory of linguistics that was quite different from the theory I espoused. My theory is called "anthropological linguistics." The theory taught at UCLA at that time may be called "theoretical linguistics" or "transformational grammar." There are many differences between these theories, among which is the fact that the theory I follow is practical and usable with real languages. Theirs is not.

Linguistics was still fun for me but not crucial. Missiology deals with life-or-death issues in relation to God's activities in human contexts. In short, when I had the choice between a career dealing with God and his activities and the fascinating study of language, I chose missiology. So I fed the one area and starved the other and the UCLA linguistics department decided they didn't need me anymore and gave me one final year (1972–73) and terminated me. But, since I had the position at Fuller, that was okay. They simply made the position full time.

CHAPTER 14

MISSIOLOGICAL WRITINGS I:
1960–1980

OTHER THAN A FEW informal things, my first professional writing for publication was my 1961 "Correspondence Courses in Anthropology," published in the important missionary anthropology journal *Practical Anthropology* (8:168–75). I was a student in my doctoral program at Hartford Seminary at the time and concerned that missionaries on the field had correspondence resources in anthropology they might not know about. I had profited while on the field by enrolling in a couple of courses and thought that this was a resource that could help with the paucity of programs available to missionaries.

CONVERSION

In 1963 I had an important article entitled "Christian Conversion or Cultural Conversion" published in *Practical Anthropology* (10:179–87). I had been concerned for some time over the fact that missions in Africa (and elsewhere) often gave the impression that converting to Christ required two conversions, one to Christ, the other to as much as possible of Western culture. I pointed to Acts

15 for scriptural support for distinguishing between converting to Christ as a part of converting to a Western religion and converting directly, without adopting the customs of another culture.

When I wrote the article, of course, I had no idea of the part it would play in my future. In 1968 when my name had been suggested as a potential faculty member of the School of World Mission, Drs. McGavran, Tippett, and Winter knew of the article and, even before they had gotten to know me, were able to refer to this article to get a feel for my views on culture and conversion. When I signed on, then, Dr. McGavran asked me to work out a course on conversion that would make use of that article. He encouraged me to further develop the approach I had outlined in the article.

In this year I also did a review article entitled "Mission in a World of Rapid Social Change" for *Practical Anthropology* (10:271–79) based on three books: Aidan Southall, *Social Change in Modern Africa*; Egbert DeVries, *Man in Rapid Social Change*; and Paul Abrecht, *The Churches and Rapid Social Change*. These were significant books for their time and I was positive toward their contribution to missiology. All three books supported my culture positive approach toward the introduction of Christianity.

COMMUNICATION

At Fuller I wrote quite a number of articles dealing in one way or another with communication.

1. The first of these was given a title that my kids had a lot of fun with. It was something like "I know you believe you understand what you think I said but I'm not sure you realize that what you heard is not what I meant." This was shortened when published to "What You Heard Is Not What I Meant," *World Vision Magazine* 13 (April 1969), 10–12. The article had to do with the miscommunication that often goes on when people of two societies interact.

2. "The New Wine of Independence," *World Vision* 15 (February 1971) 6–9, had to do with some of the complications for both

missionary and non-missionary churches in facing the challenges of gaining independence from missionary Christianity.

3. "Younger Churches—Missionaries and Indigeneity," *Church Growth Bulletin* 7 (1971) 159–61, dealt with the missionary aspects of the movement toward indigeneity.

4. I published two very significant articles on communication in 1973. These both presented communication theory as a valid part of missiology. They highlighted the incarnational approach that I had taken in my own ministry and that I was teaching and developing in my work at Fuller. The first was entitled "God's Model for Cross-Cultural Communication—the Incarnation," *Evangelical Missions Quarterly* 9 (1973) 205–16. The second article was entitled "The Incarnation, Cross-Cultural Communication and Communication Theory," *Evangelical Missions Quarterly* 9 (1973) 277–84.

5. I wrote an additional article for *Missiology* dealing with worldview and intercultural communication. The article was entitled "Ideological Factors in Intercultural Communication," *Missiology* 2 (1974) 295–312.

6. "Communicate or Compete?" *Spectrum* (Spring-Summer 1976) 8–10.

7. The Fuller publication, *Theology, News and Notes*, asked me to edit a whole issue on Bible translation. My editorial, "Bible Translation and the Church," and an article focusing on God's incarnational approach recorded in the Bible, "What Is God Trying to Do?" were published in *Theology, News and Notes* (March 1977) 9–11. The article was reprinted in *Notes on Translation* 72 (December 1978) 20–26.

8. "Biblical Principles of Communication," *Harvester* 56 (1977) 262–64, 275.

9. "Worldview in Intercultural Communication," a chapter in *Intercultural and International Communication*, ed. Fred L. Casmir (Lanham, MD: University Press of America, 1978).

FOUR CAREERS

CONTEXTUALIZATION

In addition to previously mentioned writings in contextualization I wrote the following:

1. I was working on what some consider my most important publication at this time and introduced the subject of *Christianity in Culture* (1979) with a chapter in a McGavran festschrift entitled "Toward a Christian Ethnotheology," in *God, Man and Church Growth*, ed. A. R. Tippett (Grand Rapids: Eerdmans, 1973), 109–26. Ethnotheology was the name I gave to what we now refer to as contextualized theology.

2. Another chapter written for the MGavran festschrift is entitled "Church Planters and Ethnolinguistics (226–49). Both of these were bases for chapters in *Christianity in Culture*.

3. I had introduced a class on indigeneity and this article was based on that class: "Dynamic Equivalence Churches," *Missiology* 1 (October 1973) 39–57. A point that I like to make in these articles is that good churches are to look in their cultures like good Bible translations look in their cultures. Any church that looks like the King James Version is a poor translation.

4. Working from the course on conversion that I was teaching, I published "Christian Conversion as a Dynamic Process," in *International Christian Broadcasters Bulletin* (Second Quarter 1974) 8–9, 14.

5. A paper commissioned by the publishers of *Christian Scholar's Review* that involved a trip to Chicago to meet the committee for a discussion of my article. This long article was another forerunner of my book *Christianity in Culture*. Its title was "Can Anthropological Insight Assist Evangelical Theology?," *Christian Scholar's Review* 7 (1977) 165–202. My answer was "Yes," and I tried to show how.

6. Another major article was the one I contributed to *EMQ*, who did a whole issue on contextualization. This issue signaled

the turning point for evangelicals in getting used to the term. It certainly was a major statement by Evangelicals on contextualization. My article was entitled "The Contextualization of Theology," *Evangelical Missions Quarterly* 14 (1978) 311–36.

7. In 1977 we had a conference on the homogeneous unit principle, the principle of groupness that McGavran recognized as lying behind most churches. For this conference I did the following paper, simply saying that people gravitate toward the ingroup in churchness as well as in all other areas of life. My paper was then published as "An Anthropological Apologetic for the Homogeneous Unit Principle in Missiology," *Occasional Bulletin of Missionary Research* 10 (1978) 121–26.

8. In 1978 we gathered in Glen Eyrie, Colorado, for a conference on Muslim evangelism. My contribution was "Dynamic Equivalence Churches in Muslim Society," in *The Gospel and Islam: A 1978 Compendium*, ed. Donald M. McCurry (Monrovia, CA: MARC, 1979). I talked about the possibility of groups of converts that would be similar in dynamic to first century Christian groups that we call churches.

I published a few additional articles in these years, as well as presented three lectures at Northwest Christian College. Some of the topics I dealt with were:

1. "Spinoff From the Study of Cross-Cultural Mission," in *Theology, News and Notes* 18 (October 1972) 20–23.

2. "The Hutterites and Today's Church," *Theology, News and Notes* 18 (October 1972) 15–16. I found my brief study of the Hutterites fascinating, especially the way they controlled the education of their children and the social and religious life of their communities. Though my article was probably a bit superficial, I tried to highlight things that I believe we can learn from a group that controls their culture and especially their children's education.

3. "Why Have You Come," "Why Go to the Mission Field?" and "What If I Hadn't Gone?" (3 lectures), Missions Week

Lectures, Northwest Christian College (1974). I had been asked to be the missions speaker for Northwest Christian College in Minneapolis / St. Paul and these were my topics.

The year 1979 was a big one for me. My manuscript that I had been working toward *Christianity in Culture* (Maryknoll: Orbis, 1979; 2nd ed., 2005) was accepted by Orbis after being narrowly rejected by Zondervan. I also came in second for a prize from a Catholic organization for the best book that year on a theological subject. The first prize involved money; the second prize was a nice letter saying they were sorry! I had been working on this book for several years, using it as the textbook for my Christianity and Culture course. On the basis of student responses and my own growth, then, I had put the manuscript through three major revisions and a couple of minor ones. There are missiologists who consider this to be one of the most important missiological books of the last quarter of the century.

With one of my students, Tom Wisley, we collected several writings on contextualization and produced *Readings in Dynamic Indigeneity*, ed. C .H. Kraft, with T. Wisley (Pasadena: William Carey Library, 1979). Since some of the discussion about the term "contextualization" contended that the term indigeneity was static while the term contextualization was more dynamic, we decided to use the older term but to put "dynamic" with it to point up the fact that many of us who used the older term understood that the real difference lay in whether an approach was dynamic or static rather than in whether we used the term indigeneity or contextualization. Hence the term "dynamic indigeneity." In those days one of the discussions we often had in my Indigeneity course was whether or not we could measure indigeneity. With this in mind, I wrote "Measuring Indigeneity," an article which later was published in our Readings book.

From 1980 to 1984 I published a number of things in my various fields. The first was one on the clash between Christianity and anthropology for the *Journal of the American Scientific Affiliation*, entitled "Conservative Christians and Anthropologists: A Clash of Worldviews," *JASA* 32 (September 1980) 140–45.

Then the compendium from the 1978 Willowbank Conference came out including my paper "The Church in Culture—a Dynamic Equivalence Model," in *Down to Earth: Studies in Christianity and Culture*, ed. John Stott and Robert Coote (Grand Rapids: Eerdmans, 1980). This conference may have been the only conference to that date in which theologians and anthropologists interacted. There's good stuff in that volume and the Willowbank Report has a lot of my influence in it.

CHAPTER 15

MISSIOLOGICAL WRITINGS II:
1980–2008

PUBLISHING ON TWO TRACKS

Since the paradigm shifts that I went through in 1982, I entered career four and began to publish on two tracks. I continued to publish in the areas of anthropology, communication, and contextualization. But I added a track by teaching and writing in areas of healing and spiritual warfare. This has resulted as I write in sixteen of my thirty-seven published books and several articles in the healing area.

ANTHROPOLOGY, COMMUNICATION, AND CONTEXTUALIZATION

Perhaps one of the more significant books in the 1980s was *Oral Communication of the Scripture*, by Herbert V. Klem (Pasadena: William Carey Library, 1982). It took a bit if work together on this dissertation to make it publishable. So I gladly and proudly wrote the foreword to this book. Whenever we discussed the book after its publication, Herb always referred it as "our book."

Sometime in 1981 an editor from Abingdon Press came to my office to see if I would write something for them. The upshot of our conversation was that I would write a book on communication. The result was *Communication Theory for Christian Witness* (Nashville: Abingdon, 1983). Abingdon marketed the book for several years, then let it go out of print. So, I submitted it to Orbis, who initially turned it down, but when I resubmitted it, accepted it and published a revised edition in 1991.

Also in the anthropology/communication area I wrote:

1. "Cultural Anthropology: Its Meaning for Theology," *Theology Today* 41 (1985) 390–400.

2. I wrote "Gospel and Culture" in a compendium called *Christianity in Today's World*, 274–45 (Grand Rapids: Eerdmans). Also in British edition entitled *Christianity: A World Faith* (London: Lion).

3. Foreword (with Marguerite G. Kraft), *Introduction to Missiology*, by A. R. Tippett (William Carey Library, 1987). In this book we published several of Tippett's unpublished articles and papers.

I wrote two tributes to my former colleague Alan Tippett after he passed away. "Who Was This Man" (tribute to Alan Tippett), *Missiology* 17 (July 1989) 269–81, and an article in *The Australian Dictionary of Evangelical Biography*, ed. Brian Dickey (Evangelical Historical Society, 1994).

In 1989 my colleague Dean Gilliland published a book on contextualization that several of us School of World Mission faculty were asked to write for. My contribution was "Contextualizing Communication," in *The Word Among Us*, ed. Dean Gilliland (Dallas: Word, 1989), 121–38.

Then in the Philippines OMF put out their edition of two of my books: *Christianity with Power* and *Communicate with Power*. This latter book is the same as *Communicating God's Way* but with

FOUR CAREERS

their title. *Communicate with Power* (Manila: OMF Literature, 1990); Korean translation, entitled *Jesus, God's Model for Christian Communication* (1992).

I had been thinking about the ethics of missions for my introductory anthropology course and textbook. So I submitted this article to *Transformation Magazine*, "Receptor-Oriented Ethics in Cross-Cultural Intervention," *Transformation* 8 (Jan-Mar 1991) 20–25.

I finally got my introductory anthropology book published in 1996. The book had been developed from my twenty-seven years of teaching the SWM anthropology class and I was and am proud of it. *Anthropology for Christian Witness* (Maryknoll: Orbis, 1996).

Having seen a twenty-fifth-anniversary edition of Vincent Donovan's excellent book *Christianity Rediscovered* done by Orbis, I suggested to Bill Burrows, the Orbis editor, that they consider a twenty-fifth-year edition of my *Christianity in Culture*. He thought it was a good idea, so I did a minor revision and he published it. *Christianity in Culture: A Study in Dynamic Biblical Theologizing in Cross Cultural Perspective*, with Marguerite G. Kraft, rev. 25th-year ed. (Maryknoll: Orbis, 2005).

Newt Maloney on the Fuller School of Psychology faculty asked me to do an article on conversion for the handbook he was working on. "Conversion in Group Settings," in *Handbook of Religious Conversion*, ed. Newt Maloney and Samuel Southard (Religious Education Press, 1992).

I published "Understanding and Valuing Multiethnic Diversity," with Marguerite G. Kraft, *Theology News and Notes* 40 (1993) 6–8.

In 1986 I was invited to the Dallas headquarters of Wycliffe Bible Translators / Summer Institute of Linguistics for a conference on WBT/SIL and anthropology. I was able to bring Alan Tippett back from Australia for the conference. We had a good time. I spoke on the following topics and the papers were published. "Worldview and Bible Translation," in *Anthropological and Missiological Issues, Notes on Anthropology*, ed. Karl J. Franklin (Dallas: Summer Institute of Linguistics), nos. 6 & 7, June-September,

1986, 46–57. "Missiology and SIL," in *Current Concerns of Anthropologists and Missionaries*, ed. Karl J. Franklin (Dallas: SIL, 1987), 133–42.

I did a chapter in a book edited by my friend the late Harvie Conn and others entitled "Generational Appropriateness in Contextualization," in *The Urban Face of Mission*, ed. H. Conn et al. (Phillipsburg, NJ: P&R, 2002), 132–56.

For several years I had been working on a new text on contextualization. We wanted to honor Dean Gilliland, so we dedicated the book to him. There are eighteen authors, but I wrote eleven of the chapters myself to try to cover most of the territory. The book is *Appropriate Christianity* (Pasadena, CA: William Carey Library, 2005). My chapters are the following:

"Appropriate Contextualization of Spiritual Power"
"Appropriate Relationships"
"Contextualization and Time: Generational Appropriateness"
"Contextualization in Three Crucial Dimensions"
"The Development of Contextualization Theory in Euroamerican Missiology"
"Dynamics of Contextualization"
"Is Christianity a Religion or a Faith?"
"Meaning Equivalence Contextualization"
"Spiritual Power: A Missiological Issue"
"Why Appropriate?"
"Why Isn't Contextualization Implemented?"

In 2007 I was finally able to get my worldview text published, *Worldview for Christian Witness* (Pasadena, CA: William Carey Library, 2007). This is the product of my long-standing course entitled "Worldview and Worldview Change." From early on, I taught this course with the understanding that Christian theology is a matter of worldview, not simply of surface-level doctrines. Paul Hiebert joined our faculty in 1977 and requested that we each do the course in alternate years. I sat in on Hiebert's course one year and learned a lot. I believe our interaction on worldview that year and throughout the thirteen years he was with us at SWM was helpful to both us and our students.

An article I did for the Vineyard kind of put both of my emphases together. I became convinced that the peoples of the world really need charismatic missionaries, since most peoples are on a quest for greater spiritual power. So I wrote for a Vineyard magazine: "Why the Vineyard Should Move into Cross-Cultural Ministry," *First Fruits*, November/December 1985, 15–19.

HEALING AND SPIRITUAL WARFARE

On the spiritual power side of my life, I published the following: "The 'Third Wave' in the Covenant Church," *Narthex* 5 (1985) 5–15. This was a contribution to a discussion within the Evangelical Covenant Church over the ministry of John Wimber. Since I belong to Pasadena Covenant Church, I was asked to contribute this article.

Other publications on spiritual power were the following:

1. "The Question of Miracles," *Pentecostal Minister* (Winter 1986) 24.

2. "Five Years Later," in *Signs and Wonders Today: The Remarkable Story of the MC510 Signs, Wonders and Church Growth at Fuller Theological Seminary*, ed. C. Peter Wagner (Wheaton, IL: Christian Life Magazine, 1987), 115–24. This was a discussion of the 1982–1985 events at Fuller centered around the teaching of John Wimber. The selections were by those of us most affected by what has been called the "Signs and Wonders Movement." I did a report on this movement for an Australian publication entitled "Evangelicals Rediscover the Gifts," *Renewing Australia*, December 1986, 12–13.

In 1986 a collection of articles on hermeneutics was put together by Donald McKim. It is interesting that, though hermeneutics is a normal part of the theological curriculum in the Fuller School of Theology, the only selection from Fuller, chosen by McKim was a chapter out of my *Christianity in Culture* (1979). "Supracultural Meanings via Cultural Forms," in *A Guide to*

Contemporary Hermeneutics, ed. Donald K. McKim (Grand Rapids: Eerdmans, 1986), 309–43.

I did several articles on spiritual power in 1987 and following:

1. "The World Needs More Spiritual Power," in *AD2000* (May 1987) 3.

2. "Shifting Worldviews, Shifting Attitudes," in *Riding the Third Wave*, ed. John Wimber and Kevin Springer (Basingstoke, UK: Marshall Pickering, 1987), 122–34.

I had been contemplating doing a book on worldview related to spiritual power when Servant Books asked me to do such a book. So I wrote *Christianity with Power* with the aim of helping Evangelicals to change their perspective on spiritual power as I had. Part of the book is my story. The book has been favorably received both in the United States and abroad in translation. When Servant Publications went out of business, then, Wipf & Stock reprinted it. *Christianity with Power* (Ann Arbor: Servant, 1989), now published by Wipf & Stock. It has been translated into at least four languages.

The School of World Mission students started a magazine, *Missions Tomorrow*, that unfortunately only lasted two issues. I wrote for that magazine. "Don't Worry about Ignorance: It's Our Knowledge That's the Problem," *Missions Tomorrow* (Spring/Summer 1989) 27–34. Another version of this article was published in Australia in two parts as: "It's What We Think We Know—That's the Problem," *Renewing Australia* (December 1991) 14–15, 37. And "Changing What We Know," *Renewing Australia* (June 1992) 19–21, 29.

In 1989 we did a conference at Fuller on spiritual power. Wimber was there and so were a couple of Pentecostals. A major point of discussion was whether or not Christians could be demonized. The Pentecostals were adamant that Christians could not be demonized, but there was too much experience against their position. My part in the conference was to respond to Doug Pennoyer. It was published as "Response to F. Douglas Pennoyer,"

FOUR CAREERS

in *Wrestling with Dark Angels*, ed. C. Peter Wagner and F. Douglas Pennoyer (Ventura, CA: Regal, 1990).

POWER ENCOUNTERS

Two presentations of my Three Encounters concept came out in 1991 and 1992. The first has been referred to here in several places and became the precursor of my Three Crucial Dimensions presentations in more recent writings.

1. "What Kind of Encounters Do We Need in our Christian Witness?," *Evangelical Missions Quarterly* 27 (1991) 258–65.

2. "Allegiance, Truth and Power Encounters in Christian Witness," in *Pentecost, Mission and Ecumenism: Essays on Intercultural Theology*, ed. Jan. A. B. Jongeneel (New York: Lang, 1992).

3. "The Concept of Power Encounter," *CMS Bulletin* 3.2:1–2.

4. "Taking Out the Garbage and Exterminating the Rats," *Renewal News for Presbyterian and Reformed Churches* (Summer, 1994).

One of my favorite articles was commissioned by Gary Greig for his book on the kingdom. Meg and I did it together, starting with a story of a demon saying to an East African Catholic priest that they (the demons) would beat him because the Christians have been riding two horses. The article is "Communicating and Ministering the Power of the Gospel Cross-Culturally: The Power of God for Christians Who Ride Two Horses," with Marguerite G. Kraft, in *The Kingdom and the Power*, ed. Gary S. Greig and Kevin N. Springer (Ventura, CA: Regal, 1993), 346–56.

Tom McAlpine of World Vision was asked by someone to do a review of the Third Wave. He did a typical academic review and probably talked some people out of moving into spiritual power. My review of his article was "Review of *Facing the Powers: What Are the Options?*, by Thomas H. McAlpine," *Missiology—An International Review*, April 1993.

114

After the success of *Christianity with Power*, Servant Books asked me to write two more books, one on inner healing, and the other on dealing with demons. I asked them which they wanted first. They said the one on demonization would probably attract more readers. So I did that one first with the help of some of my team members. *Defeating Dark Angels* (Grand Rapids: Chosen/Baker, 1992/2011). The second book Servant Books commissioned me to write was *Deep Wounds, Deep Healing* (Grand Rapids: Chosen/Baker, 1993/2000). When Servant Books went out of business in 2000, Regal took it over. Baker has taken over these books. They have sold well. Both have been translated into at least five languages.

Spinning off from the section on spiritual power that I coordinated at the Lausanne meetings in Manila in 1989 was the following edited book. Mine was the second-best attended session at that conference, saying something about the interest in spiritual power among Evangelicals. Papers presented at these meetings were published in *Behind Enemy Lines*, ed. Charles H. Kraft (Ann Arbor, MI: Servant, 1994; repr. Wipf & Stock, 2000). My chapters in this book are "Two Kingdoms in Conflict," "Spiritual Power: Principles and Observations," and "Dealing with Demonization." This book was translated into three languages.

David DeBord and I decided to enlarge the chapter in *Behind Enemy Lines* that deals with the rules and principles in terms of which the human and supernatural worlds interrelate and came up with *The Rules of Engagement: Understanding the Principles That Govern the Spiritual Battles in Our Lives*, with David M. DeBord (Colorado Springs: Wagner, 2000; repr. Wipf & Stock). I am convinced that there is a science dealing with this interaction and I have tried to list and discuss some of the principles.

In the Evangelical Missiological Society meeting of 1994, a paper was presented that attacked those of us who had moved into spiritual power. We had no warning of this but when we found it out and read the paper, Wagner and I determined to answer the charges. Peter wrote a book called *Confronting the Powers*. I responded in a paper that was published along with the original attack in a volume called *Spiritual Power and Missions*. I called it "'Christian Animism' or God-Given Authority," in *Spiritual Power and Missions*, ed. Edward Rommen (Pasadena, CA: William Carey Library, 1995), 88–136. The authors of this attack demonstrated that they didn't know the difference between animism and authority. They accused us of practicing what they called "Christian animism" and seemed to imply that all power ministry is empowered by Satan. Though I resented the time it took to reply to them as well as the way they presented the paper, the exercise did me good in helping me to define some of the issues in the debate.

I had been working on a book on authority. Writing this book was a challenge, more difficult than most of my books, but the results were gratifying, leading some to consider it my best book. *I Give You Authority* (Grand Rapids: Baker/Chosen, 1997). It has been translated into four or five different languages.

Then it was my turn to write my pilgrimage story for the *International Bulletin of Missionary Research*. It was an honor to be asked to write my story and I embraced it. "My Pilgrimage in Mission," *International Bulletin of Missionary Research* 22 (October 1998) 162–64.

I was asked to write an article for the Perspectives textbook on culture and contextualization and to allow my Three Encounters article to be reprinted in the 1999 revision of the Perspectives textbook. "Culture, Worldview and Contextualization," in *Perspectives on the World Christian Movement* (Pasadena, CA: William Carey Library, 1999), 384–91.

I was asked to write ten articles in the *Evangelical Dictionary of World Mission*, ed. A. Scott Moreau, Charles Van Engen, and Harold A. Netland (Baker, 2000). The articles are:

1. "Anthropology," *EDWM*, pp. 66–68.

2. "Cultural Conversion," *EDWM*, p. 251.

3. "Culture Shock," *EDWM*, pp. 256–57.

4. "Curse, Curses," *EDWM*, pp. 257–58.

5. "Divination, Diviners," *EDWM*, p. 282.

6. "Dynamic Equivalence," *EDWM*, p. 295.

7. "Interpersonal Communication," *EDWM*, pp. 499–500.

8. "Polygamy and Church Membership," *EDWM*, p. 766.

9. "Power Encounter," *EDWM*, pp. 774–75.

10. "Witchcraft and Sorcery," *EDWM*, pp. 1019–20.

Because students frequently asked me about things I have written that were hard to find, I assigned my teaching assistant David Bjork to copy articles and chapters in books toward the publication in 2001 of *Culture, Communication and Christianity: A Selection of Writings by Charles H. Kraft* (Pasadena, CA: William Carey Library, 2001). Though most of the chapters are previously published materials, it includes four new articles. These are:

1. "Anthropological Perspectives on American Women's Issues." For two years in the seventies the Fuller women had asked me to teach a course just for them, entitled "God, Culture and Women." This paper came out of that course and had not been published previously.

2. "Let's Be Christian about Polygamy." I had written this in my Hartford days to make my position clear but had never gotten it published.

3. "The Bearing of the Passages in 1 Timothy and Titus on the Matter of Church Leadership in Polygamous Societies." I wrote this paper also in my Hartford days as a follow-up to the preceding article.

4. "God, Human Beings, Culture and the Cross-Cultural Communication of the Gospel." This was the chapter I wrote for McGavran's book *Crucial Issues* but it was rejected.

I was asked by Doris Wagner to contribute to her book dealing with demonic oppression. I was surprised at this, given that we disagree on whether or not to talk to demons. I mentioned this to her but she invited me to write the chapter anyway. My chapter was entitled "The Believer's Authority over Demonic Spirits," in

Ministering Freedom from Demonic Oppression, ed. Doris M. Wagner (Colorado Springs: Wagner, 2002), 43–63; reprinted in *How to Minister Freedom*, ed. D. M. Wagner (Ventura, CA: Regal), 50–59.

The publication of my presentations at the Deliver Us from Evil conference in Nairobi were published in *Deliver Us from Evil*, ed. A. S. Moreau et al. (Monrovia, CA: MARC, 2002), 290–308. My papers were "Contemporary Trends in the Treatment of Spiritual Conflict" and "Contextualization and Spiritual Power."

I had several things on spiritual power that I hadn't published. So I put them together to make another book, titled *Confronting Powerless Christianity* (Grand Rapids: Baker/Chosen, 2002). One of the chapters is the paper that the Fuller faculty had asked me to write to be discussed in plenary session. We had four sessions, supposedly discussing the place of spiritual power at Fuller. The faculty completely ignored my paper and I was thoroughly disappointed in their reaction. Other chapters included are on three-dimensional Christianity (relationship, truth, and spiritual power), on partnership (God usually requires that there be a human partner if he is to work in the human arena), and on the fact that freedom is for most people a step beyond salvation (it doesn't usually come with salvation) followed by an outline of spiritual warfare.

In 2006 my three dimensions concept was published in Australia, "Christianity in Three Crucial Dimensions," in *Speaking of Mission*, ed. Michael Frost (Sydney: Morling, 2006).

I was asked to write a history of the School of World Mission for our fortieth anniversary since I had been here for all but the first four years of SWM's existence. This I did with a focus on the people who made up the faculty and staff of the school. I did a chapter dealing with the future, suggesting that we need to find a focus around which to rally. In the early days we had church growth as our core. I suggested that incarnational ministry might be a good focus for today. *SWM/SIS at Forty* (Pasadena, CA: William Carey Library, 2005).

WORSHIP LEADER MAGAZINE

I was asked by my good friend Chuck Fromm (owner and editor of *Worship Leader* magazine) to write a column focusing on worship and communication. There were thirty-three of these from 1992 to 1999. Among them were

1. "Hymns vs. Praise Songs: Which Shall We Sing?"

2. "How Our Worldview Affects the Way We Worship"

3. "Communication in Worship: To Whom Do We Sing?"

4. "Our Youth Need to Know That Worship Is Warfare"

5. "How Acts of Worship Help Defeat the Devil"

6. "Worship: Tradition, or Just 'Follow the Leader'?"

7. "Traditions Too Often Lose Meaning over Time"

I had a lot of fun doing it. My favorite article, "Organ or Guitar?" asks the question, "Can you picture Jesus playing an organ? How about a guitar?" Later I published twenty-five of these articles in a book called *Worship beyond the Hymnal* (Eugene, OR: Wipf & Stock, 2015).

In 1986, Donald Hustad wrote a piece in *Christianity Today* that was critical of contemporary worship music and decried the rejection of hymnals. "How will future generations of young people get to know the rich spiritual heritage recorded in the hymnal if we turn completely to contemporary praise and worship songs?" Hustad asked. Chuck Fromm pointed out the article to me and asked if I would write a rejoinder. This I did and submitted it to *Christianity Today* but it was rejected. One of the major points I tried to make in the article that was turned down is that our young people will not likely learn to love the old hymns at all if that's all we offer them, since they won't be coming to church. We need the new music to attract them. Then we will have the chance to expose them to the riches of the hymns along with the new music. However, *CT* did invite me to write a very short piece on the subject.

This was published as "The Hymnal Is Not Enough," *Christianity Today*, April 7, 1989, 8.

I'd like to mention one more book which though not written by me was written for me. It is a custom in academic circles when a professor is to be specially honored, for colleagues to write a book for him or her. This book is called a Festschrift. See the next chapter.

CHAPTER 16

RETIREMENT

IN 2008 IT WAS decided that I should teach one more course, Worldview and Worldview Change, then be done with teaching at Fuller. For a couple of years I tried to keep up by attending the Tuesday noon SIS faculty meetings. But it was not the same. My teaching days at the School of Intercultural Studies were over, except for an occasional invite to teach a class.

After spending forty-one years on the Fuller faculty I see my contribution to missiology in continuing the pioneering efforts of McGavran and Tippett on one hand and Eugene Nida and his worthy associates of the 1950s and 1960s on the other. Much of the latters' written record of their (and my) approach was published in the journal *Practical Anthropology.* I have been privileged to have a hand in the development of missionary anthropology, the harnessing of communication theory for Christian mission, and the acceptance and development of contextualization theory by Evangelicals. I also have pioneered the importance of dealing with spiritual power in missionary training and practice. These and other contributions are documented in my writings. The opportunity to teach and write in missiology these many years has been more than I could ever have hoped for in life. I never planned my life this way but am amazed at what God has done with me.

FOUR CAREERS

When I prepared to move out of my Fuller office, I was pondering what to do with my books and papers when the Fuller librarian asked if he could have my things to place in an archive in the Fuller library. This surprised me, especially when he gave the reason for his interest. He said, "Someday someone will want to study you. We need these materials to make that possible." Though I can't imagine why someone would want to study me, I've given the Fuller Seminary library nearly all my stuff (mostly books and papers) for whatever anyone wants to make of it.

FURTHER WRITING

In retirement I have continued my writing, especially in the area of spiritual power. I published *Two Hours to Freedom* (Grand Rapids: Chosen/Baker, 2010). It is a short introduction to inner healing the way I practice it. I make my appointments for two hours and go through a three-step process: getting acquainted, inner healing, deliverance. The book sets out this approach plus some fairly new information on memories.

An additional publication is my revision of *Deep Wounds, Deep Healing* by Regal in 2010. I next revised *Defeating Dark Angels* for Regal for a 2011 publication. Both of these books were picked up by Chosen/Baker when Regal folded.

I published a new book, *The Evangelical's Guide to Spiritual Warfare* (Grand Rapids: Chosen/Baker, 2015). Though much of the material in this book leans heavily on what I've written in other places, this is my present statement on that subject.

In 2016 I published *Issues in Contextualization* (Pasadena: William Carey Library), focusing on an "insider" approach to communicating and expressing the gospel. It is important for all peoples to experience a Christianity that is theirs, not one transplanted from another culture with their forms and Christian meanings.

Next came *Power Encounter in Spiritual Warfare* (2017) and *Dealing with Demons* (Eugene, OR: Wipf & Stock, 2018). In 2019 I published *Satan Is Afraid You Will Discover Your True Identity: Do You Know Who You Are?* (Chosen/Baker).

RETIREMENT BANQUET

On the evening of March 12, 2008, the School of Intercultural Studies put on a very nice retirement banquet for me. They invited our whole family, grandkids and all, my sister Sharon from New Hampshire, and several other people who have meant a lot to me over the years. They also scheduled a mini-conference on contextualization for the next morning where papers were presented and I was asked to respond.

Nice things were said by my Fuller colleagues Betty Sue Brewster, Tim Park, Roberta King, Dean Gilliland, Chuck Van Engen, and also by Darrell Whiteman, who had flown in from Atlanta, and Bill Burrows, the senior editor of Orbis Publishers, who have published three of my books, came in from New York. And Chuck Van Engen presented me with a Festschrift, named *Paradigm Shifts in Christian Witness*, ed. Chuck Van Engen, Darrell Whiteman, and Dudley Woodberry (Orbis, 2008).

That sister Sharon from New Hampshire was there was a complete surprise to me. The tables full of our kids (all four, plus spouses) and grandkids (13 of 15 were there) made quite an impression on many. The grandkids did a song for me, Kimberly Martell spoke of her grandpa, and Meg gave a tribute also. Son Rick spoke eloquently, as did the others who spoke. They all spoke as if I am famous. Indeed, nine-year-old Andrew Schneider asked his parents (Karen and Bruce) on the way home, "Is grandpa famous?"

THE FESTSCHRIFT: PARADIGM SHIFTS

Over the years I have been known as one who leads students into paradigm shifts—changes in perspective. I had this reputation even before 1982 concerning my advocacy of a culture-friendly approach to mission. I treated anthropology and communication as perspectives rather than simply courses, advocating that missionaries work within, not against, the cultural ways of life of the peoples we seek to bring into the kingdom. For many of our students, this required one or more paradigm shifts.

Then, following 1982 I became known as a paradigm shifter from powerless Christianity to power-oriented Christianity. Whether in my classes or in other contexts I came to be known as a strong advocate for dealing with spiritual power issues in missiology. For many of my students and the readers of my books this was a stretch. But many have survived the paradigm shift and become advocates and practitioners of power ministry. In fact, some have found that an increased focus on spiritual power has transformed their ministry.

Given my history, then, it was appropriate that any Festschrift for me have "paradigm shift" in the title. Accordingly, colleagues/ editors put together, under the title *Paradigm Shifts in Christian Witness*, a well-done tribute to my contributions in three areas of missiology: anthropology, communication, and spiritual power (however, they overlooked contextualization). The authors of the chapters are former students (Roberta King, Viggo Sogaard, and Knud Jorgensen), esteemed colleagues (the late Paul Hiebert, Darrell Whiteman, Robert Priest, Michael Rynkiewich, Chuck Van Engen, Paul Pierson, Doug McConnell, Dan Shaw, Dean Gilliland, Peter Wagner, Dudley Woodberry, Robert Schreiter, and Tormod Engelsviken), my "guru," the late Eugene Nida, and a couple of protégés, John and Anna Travis.

I am greatly honored to have a book written to commemorate my work over forty-plus years at Fuller. Van Engen did the preface to the book. Among other things, he suggests that there is a "Before Kraft and After Kraft Missiology" and that my work in the three areas in focus has brought about significant paradigm shifts in the next generation of missiologists. Whether or not that is true will be up to the historians to decide someday. As for me, I am extremely honored to have an esteemed colleague speak of me in that way.

In introductory chapters Van Engen, McConnell, Pierson, and Shaw surveyed my life and ministry. They have many nice things to say about me and I am grateful to them.

Then the book turns to dealing with the important place of anthropology in missiology, a cause that I have championed for my whole career. There are chapters by four prominent Christian anthropologists. Whiteman edited this section and wrote of the uneasy relationship between anthropology and mission. Priest also reflected on that relationship, Rynkiewich spoke of the future of missiological anthropology. Then the greatest of us all, the late Paul Hiebert, who in the last days of his life honored me with his contribution dealing with epistemological shifts required when missiology and anthropology meet.

The second section of the book, then, focused on the importance of communication insight to missiology. Van Engen edited this section as well as the whole volume. Perhaps my importance in this area is displayed by the fact that three of the four authors were my students, and two of them became SIS faculty. They are the late Viggo Sogaard who surveyed the principles of incarnational communication that I had focused on, King who wrote on the relationship of communication to missiology and the late Knud Jorgensen who focused on communication theory and its place in missiology. The fourth author, then, was the late Eugene Nida. His chapter is a general one with pieces from various of his writings that Van Engen put together and got approved by Nida before he died. I am honored both for the content of these chapters and for the mark that these have made on missiology.

The third section, then, deals with my involvement in spiritual power. Woodberry, who has emphasized the importance of focusing on spiritual power in dealing with Muslims, honored me with one chapter and edited that section. My former colleague and fellow healer, the late Peter Wagner, wrote on the need for missiology to deal with spiritual power. John and Anna Travis are protégés of mine and have adequately taken over my spiritual dynamics courses at Fuller. They wrote on deep-level healing. Engelsviken wrote the final chapter on the challenge to the church of dealing with spiritual conflict.

The mini-seminar they held the day following the banquet was good also and honored me in another way. Bill Burrows, Darrell Whiteman, and Dudley Woodberry presented papers and I did a response. The theme of the consultation was the role of the social sciences in missiology. The mini-consultation was a fitting ending to the retirement celebration.

FURTHER MINISTRY

In addition to writing I have continued to focus more on ministering to people to bring them spiritual and emotional freedom. For several years I had an office where with my very capable colleague, Judy Taber, we continued an inner healing and deliverance ministry, called Kraft Ministries. There we ministered to people one-on-one to bring them freedom. We also did a lot of teaching seminars and workshops from that office. I have ministered to literally hundreds of people.

It has been gratifying to reflect on the way God has used this ministry. I often hear from people whose lives have been changed. In addition to changed lives, some have started their own ministries in the United States and abroad as spin-offs from my ministry. It is humbling when I see what great things God has done.

FAMILY

As I write my story, I need to call attention to those who have traveled with me—my family. First, my wife, Marguerite, who has been with me as wife since 1953, as girlfriend since 1949. We have had a long time together, a tribute to her patience. She was always in the background, carrying the heaviest load with our kids while I was making a name for myself—positive in many circles, negative in some. I thank her with all my heart for sticking in there with me, even when I embarrassed her by coloring outside the lines.

I am thankful also that we made the decision for her to gain credentials so she could have her own career. As noted, she was able to get her MA from Hartford in 1963 when I received my PhD. As I was teaching at Fuller, then, she was able to take advantage of Fuller's policy to allow faculty members to study for free. So she worked hard and earned a DMiss (doctor of missiology), and eventually a PhD in intercultural studies to give her more flexibility in her ability to supervise doctoral research. So we call her a "paradox" (pair of docs). This equipped her to have a career of her own, independent of me now that the kids are on their own. She spent thirty-one years teaching missionaries and other cross-cultural workers in the School of Intercultural Studies at Biola University.

Just a word about the others who have walked this path with me. Our four children have been troopers as we have made many moves and adjustments. We do more things with the family now than we could have before retirement. Each of our children have married and given us a total of fifteen grandchildren and so far sixteen great grandchildren. Our house is big and they all enjoy coming here to monthly birthday parties (sometimes celebrating five or six birthdays at a time). My family is special and a clear sign of God's great blessing.

CONCLUDING THOUGHTS

Following Jesus has been a wonderful adventure, whether it's been as missionary, as church planter, as missiologist, or as one enabling missionaries to function with an incarnational, culture-affirming approach.

My aim as a missionary serving in a Nigerian village was to express their relationship to Christ in ways appropriate to their culture. And now, over fifty years later, the estimate is that the whole tribal group of between 500,00 and a million is 95 percent Christian. The message had come to them in appropriate ways as an "insider" thing and they responded big time. Christianity is now theirs, in their cultural forms. "As the Father has sent me, so I send you" (John 20:21).

Even the decade as a linguist in the secular setting functioned to enhance the cause of missions. I met regularly with cross-cultural workers informally to deal with language and cultural issues in communicating the gospel. Whether in a secular or Christian context I trust that living my faith has given honor to my Lord.

One of the things God brought into clear focus for me was the importance of understanding and working in Holy Spirit power. One of the most important of my emphases is the place of spiritual power in Christian experience. It has been a real blessing to see captives set free. The place of spiritual power in Christian witness and missiology is appropriate to incarnational ministry. God has used this to transform people in churches and in ministries.

I never planned to be anything but a field missionary but God made me a missiologist helping cross-cultural workers be more effective in the Christian cause. I have focused on the how of mission as well as the content. I tried to encourage missionaries to work as cultural insiders in this post-colonial era. Whether I have been successful or not will be left to historians.

It has been fun and challenging at times. May God bless my effort. It has been gratifying to note the positive response expressed by many students and colleagues to my teaching and writing. Many tell me that they are now more effective in ministry. To God be the glory.

BIBLIOGRAPHY
OF WORKS CITED

Abrecht, Paul. *The Churches and Rapid Social Change*. London: SCM, 1961.

Cassidy, Michael and Luc Verlinden. *Facing the New Challenges: The Message of PACLA*. Nairobi, Kenya: Evangel Publishing House, 1978.

Conn, Harvie M. *Eternal Word and Changing Worlds: Theology, Anthropology, and Mission in Trialogue*. Grand Raids, MI: Zondervan, 1984.

Devries, Egbert. *Man in Rapid Social Change*. Garden City, NY: Doubleday, 1961.

Donovan, Vincent J. *Christianity Rediscovered*. Maryknoll, NY: Orbis, 1978.

Kato, Byang. *Theological Pitfalls in Africa*. Kisumu, Kenya: Evangel Publishing House, 1975.

Kraft, Charles H. *Anthropology for Christian Witness*. Maryknoll, NY: Orbis, 1996.

———. *Christianity in Culture: Study in Dynamic Biblical Theologizing in Crosscultural Perspective*. Maryknoll, NY: Orbis, 1979.

———. *Confronting Powerless Christianity*. Grand Rapids: Chosen/Baker, 2002.

———. *Culture, Communication and Christianity: A Selection of Writings*. Pasadena, CA: William Carey Library, 2001.

Kraft, Charles H. (with T. N. Wisley). *Readings in Dynamic Indigeneity*. Pasadena, CA: William Carey Library, 1979.

Nida, Eugene A. *Customs and Cultures: Anthropology for Christian Missions*. New York: Harper & Brothers, 1954.

McGavran, Donald Anderson. *The Bridges of God: A Study in the Strategy of Missions*. Rev. and enlarged ed. New York: Friendship Press, 1981. Original edition, 1955.

Southall, Aidan. *Social Change in Modern Africa*. London: Oxford University Press, 1961.

www.ingramcontent.com/pod-product-compliance
Lightning Source LLC
Chambersburg PA
CBHW060356090426
42734CB00011B/2151